ENHANCING
THINKING SKILLS
IN THE
SCIENCES AND MATHEMATICS

ENHANCING THINKING SKILLS IN THE SCIENCES AND MATHEMATICS

Edited by

DIANE F. HALPERN
California State University
San Bernardino

LEA

LAWRENCE ERLBAUM ASSOCIATES, PUBLISHERS
1992   Hillsdale, New Jersey   Hove and London

Lawrence Erlbaum Associates, Inc., Publishers
365 Broadway
Hillsdale, New Jersey 07642

Library of Congress Cataloging-in-Publication Data
Enhancing thinking skills in the sciences and mathematics / edited by
   Diane F. Halpern.
      p.   cm.
   Includes bibliographical references and indexes.
   ISBN 0-8058-1052-8 (cloth). — ISBN 0-8058-1053-6 (paper)
      1. Science—Study and teaching.   2. Mathematics—Study and
teaching.   3. Creative thinking.   4. Cognition.   I. Halpern, Diane F.
Q181.E633   1992
501'.9—dc20   91-31954
                                                           CIP
Printed in the United States of America
10 9 8 7 6 5 4 3 2 1

Contents

Preface

Isaac Asimov, the prolific science fiction author, recently reported a horrifying tale. Unlike his most famous work, this particular tale is true. It is based on a random telephone survey conducted by the Public Opinion Laboratory at Northern Illinois University (Asimov, 1989). Twenty-one percent of the over 2,000 adults who responded to the survey believe that the sun revolves around the Earth, and an additional 7% do not know which revolves around which.

Consider the implications of such scientific illiteracy. It is over 400 years since the scientific community unanimously determined that the Earth revolves around the sun. It is reasonable to assume that most of the adults who responded to the survey have had basic science classes at some point in their education. How can so many Americans be ignorant of this basic fact? The answer must lie, in part, with the way science is taught and learned (or not learned) in school.

Similar surveys of the level of mathematical illiteracy are equally disturbing. Lochhead (1983) found that only 27% of *first-year engineering students* can solve word problems like this one:

> Write an equation using the variables C and S to represent the following statement: "At Mindy's restaurant, for every four people who order cheesecake, there are five people who order strudel." Let C represent the number of cheesecakes and S represent the number of strudels ordered. (p. 56)

The quality of life in North America and other industrialized parts of the world depends on a technologically enlightened citizenry. The Geosciences Workshop of the National Science Foundation (1989) concluded: ". . . inadequate precollege instruction, declining enrollments, deteriorating instructional facilities and lack of funding for research efforts involving students are particularly evident" (p. 3). Several times a year for the last several years, national and international reports are issued that decry the sad state of education and the desperate need for reform in the sciences and mathematics. We have been described as a "nation at risk" with the need to restore "integrity in the curriculum." Cognitive psychologists and mathematics and science educators have responded to this need by designing instructional programs that are more compatible with our knowledge of how people acquire, use, and retain knowledge. Many of the guiding principles that underlie these programs are presented in this volume.

I am especially pleased to serve as editor of this volume because of the outstanding quality of the contributed chapters and because of my respect for the other chapter authors. It is hoped that this book will provide valuable information about teaching and learning to professors in the sciences and mathematics and to their students.

REFERENCES

Asimov, I. (1989, March 31). Combatting U.S. scientific illiteracy. *Los Angeles Times, Part V,* 8.

Lochhead, J. (1983). The mathematical needs of students in the physical sciences. In A. Ralston & G. S. Young (Eds.), *The future of college mathematics* (pp. 55–70). New York: Springer-Verlag.

National Science Foundation. (1989). *Report on the National Science Foundation disciplinary workshops on undergraduate education.* Washington, DC: Author.

This book is dedicated to the next generation of scientists and mathematicians—the ones who will solve the problem of world hunger, discover cures for dreaded diseases, preserve the environment, and travel to distant planets—and to their teachers—the dedicated professionals who have the faith and vision to believe that all of this and more is possible.

1 A Cognitive Approach to Improving Thinking Skills in the Sciences and Mathematics

Diane F. Halpern
California State University, San Bernardino

The conclusions from several national and international studies conducted by blue ribbon panels all agree that there is a crisis in contemporary science and mathematics education. Steen (1987), for example, reported that mathematical achievement among the top 5% of 12th graders is lower in the United States than in any other industrialized nation in the world and that 8th graders in the United States are below international norms in solving problems that require higher order thinking skills. "Indeed, as the 'back-to-basics' movement has flourished in the last 15 years, the ability of U. S. students to think (rather than just to memorize) has declined accordingly" (p. 251). Similar abysmal conclusions about scientific thinking skills and knowledge based on data from 1.4 million students were recently published by the Educational Testing Service: "The majority of high-school graduates are unable to understand 'relatively complicated' information, use basic algebra, or evaluate the appropriateness of scientific procedures" (De Loughry, 1989, p. A2).

The future of the United States economy depends on our ability to maintain leadership in the development of new technologies. As a nation we not only need competent scientists and engineers, we also need a citizenry that is literate in scientific and mathematical issues so that they can vote intelligently about topics that range from acid rain to AIDS testing. Despite the increasing need for citizens educated in science and mathematics, virtually all undergraduate degree programs in the sciences and mathematics report severe declines in enrollment. A national shortage of 500,000 scientists is projected by 2010 (McMillen, 1989). We are facing serious shortages in science and mathematics teachers at all levels of education with women and many ethnic minorities woefully underrepresented.

Recent reports by the National Science Foundation (1989) and the National

Research Council (1989) echo what educators in science and mathematics have long known—there is an acute need to improve teaching and learning in these areas. Cognitive psychologists and other educators have begun to respond to this need by designing instructional programs that focus on the acquisition and use of thinking skills that are needed to find and solve mathematical and scientific problems.

THINKING AND LEARNING SKILLS

All thinking and learning skills instruction is based on two related assumptions: (a) There are thinking and learning skills that students can learn to recognize and apply appropriately; and (b) if these skills are recognized and applied, students become more effective thinkers. There are many fundamental thinking skills that are needed for successful scientific and mathematical reasoning. A general list of such skills includes, for example, understanding how cause is determined, recognizing and criticizing assumptions, analyzing means–goals relationships, assessing degrees of likelihood and uncertainty, incorporating isolated data into a wider framework, and using analogies to solve problems (Halpern, 1987a, 1987b, 1989b).

It is important to keep in mind that thinking and learning skills are developmental in nature with higher level skills building on more basic ones. Thus, whatever level a particular student is at, she or he can make cognitive gains by expanding and elaborating on a skills repertoire. A skills approach to science and mathematics education is beneficial to all students because of its emphasis on cognitive growth.

Writing and Symbol Manipulation as a Strategy for Skills Development

One general strategy for improving student proficiency in thinking and learning skills is to require both writing and symbol manipulation in every course. Mathematics courses, for example, tend to rely too heavily on rote applications of formulas. Here is a problem that I have used frequently with college students:

> Carole can mow the lawn in two hours. It takes her sister Stacy four hours. How long will it take them if they mow the lawn together?

A majority of college students have no apparent trouble with this problem. They immediately add two plus four, divide by two, and conclude that it will take them three hours if they work together. According to this answer, it will take them longer to work together than if Carole had worked alone. They rarely stop to think about their answer or the use of the formula for finding an average, which they routinely applied.

What went wrong? It is not surprising that many college students have difficulty solving this problem. What is troublesome is that so many get it wrong exactly the same way. In fact, the situation is even worse. When this problem is presented to students who have completed a course in statistics, many will set the problem up with the use of the Greek letter *mu*. Thus, after a course in statistics, they are now able to get it wrong in Greek as well as in English! This is hardly anyone's idea of a satisfactory educational outcome.

Here is a problem that many 13-year-olds have difficulty solving:

"An army bus holds 36 soldiers. If 1,128 soldiers are being bused to their training site, how many buses are needed?" (Chance, 1986, p. 26)

Most 13-year-olds have no trouble carrying out the computations involved. The problem comes in using the answer in a meaningful way. Many round the answer they receive to the nearest whole number and conclude that 31 buses are needed. Others give a decimal answer (31.33) or show the remainder from their long division. The problem is not one of basic computational skills, but of thinking about the kind of answer that the problem requires and using a strategy that is different from the one taught in school, namely rounding "up" to the next highest number rather than rounding to the nearest whole number.

Errors like these would not happen if students were required to write about the rationale and procedures before they began solving mathematical problems. All problem solving should begin with an explicit written or oral statement about the size and type of answer that would be correct (i.e., a number less than 2 for the first problem and a whole number for the second problem). It is a relatively simple matter to plug numbers into an equation and a much more difficult one to understand when and why a particular equation is applicable and what the answer means when the equation is solved. These skills can be fostered in many ways. Teachers can "think aloud" during instruction and thereby model the use of these skills. Class and homework assignments can be done in pairs or small groups in which each student thinks aloud as she or he works on problems. This approach encourages students to discuss the *solution process* rather than just the concentrating on "getting the correct answer." It also promotes active involvement in and a cooperative approach to problem solving.

In Treisman's (1985) award-winning study of ethnic differences in attitudes toward and the study of mathematics, he found that Asian-Americans, a group known for high-level participation in the natural sciences, tended to study in small groups. A number of benefits accrue from a group approach. Perhaps, most fundamentally, it tends to increase time on task—that is students spend more time on their mathematics assignments when they work with peers than when they work alone. There is also group support and informal coaching of the poorer students by the better students who model the process of solving problems. Immediate feedback on errors and faulty strategies is also a likely outcome of group problem solving. Success at mathematical problem solving builds self confidence, which in turn leads to more success. A cooperative approach to learning has many potential benefits and can easily be incorporated in any classroom.

Diagramming or other abstract representations are needed in courses that are primarily verbal. Verbal and schematic descriptions should be used to supplement each other. For example, students can "map" the structure of a chapter in a science (or other) text giving them a spatial representation of a language medium. Concept or cognitive maps can be useful in many contexts. Consider the concept map in Fig. 1.1, which depicts a student's knowledge of information about AIDS. Note the number of facts and the way the facts are linked. Maps like these can be constructed both before and after instruction on a particular topic. Comparisons of before and after concept maps can highlight instruction-related gains in knowledge. The "after instruction" maps should not only show more "facts," but should also be more differentiated with a more complex organization that represents changes in the way the information is organized. Concept maps

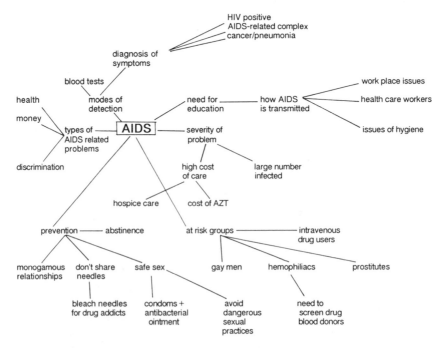

FIG. 1.1. An example of the structure and content of a student's knowledge of AIDS as seen in a concept map.

created by students (i.e., novices) can be compared with those done by experts in a field to "see" differences in the structure of knowledge. In other words, experts not only have more knowledge than novices, they also organize the information differently than novices. A complex structure of knowledge about any topic shows that students will be more likely to be able to recall and utilize the information in a wide variety of situations because there are more available recall cues. Concept maps are also useful tools for beginning writing assignments as they offer a nonlinear alternative to outlines and can be used to predict where errors occur—faulty groupings, wrong information, and skimpy structures.

The use of concept maps and writing assignments is based on cognitive theories of how people acquire and use information. They place emphasis on the relationships among topics rather than isolated "bits" of information and de-emphasize memorizing labels and lists. The use of concept maps is in accord with recent recommendations for teaching and learning science that stress fundamental principles and relationships rather than rote recitations of lists and definitions (e.g., the parts of the microscope, the parts of the cell, the names of the facial nerves, etc.).

A PROBLEM-SOLVING APPROACH

Students at all levels of education are expected to acquire information and recall it at some later time, discover and solve novel problems, evaluate the strength and nature of evidence, use reasons to support conclusions, recognize propaganda and other persuasive techniques, consider likely outcomes of actions, and question bogus claims. Yet, they are rarely taught how. Most postsecondary instruction involves transmitting facts to students with very little emphasis on how to discover the facts on their own or when to question them. Of course, the facts are important. No one can reason effectively about genetics, for example, without understanding the structure and nature of DNA. But facts change, and they often change quickly in the natural sciences. The twin abilities of how to acquire information and how to use that information to think effectively will provide the best education for today's college students—the citizens of the 21st century. One way to encourage inquisitive and creative scientists, mathematicians, and engineers is by fostering a problem-solving attitude.

For students, the two words most dreaded in the English language has got to be WORD PROBLEMS. Students often complain that they have no idea how to begin or "what to do" when they face a novel word problem. Suggestions for how to approach novel problems of all sorts can be useful because they allow students to become engaged in the problem-solving process even when their initial response is "I can't solve that." It is an intuitively obvious and often overlooked fact that the student who persists in working on a difficult problem is more likely to solve it correctly than one who gives up quickly or refuses to attempt a solution. The fact is, trying helps, but we do not always know ahead of time how it will help. Therefore, it is important to teach the habits and attitudes needed to try and try hard. General guidelines for how to approach and solve problems are especially relevant in the sciences and mathematics because students in these disciplines are more often required to find answers than to recall them.

The proposed problem-solving framework is an adaptation of the procedures originally published by the brilliant mathematician and scholar George Polya (1945). This framework is developed more fully in a recent text (Halpern, 1989b).

What Is the Goal?

The first step in improving problem solving is a clear understanding of the desired goal or end state. Unlike most classroom problems, real-life problems tend to be messy. Sometimes there are multiple goals. By contrast, most classroom problems are well-defined, that is there is a single correct answer (e.g., How much heat is generated when power is supplied at the rate of .4 hp for 2 minutes in drilling a hole in a 1-pound iron block?). Ill-defined applied problems can have several goals and the real skill lies in determining which of several possible outcomes is most desirable (e.g., How can you best design and build a bridge over a narrow rapidly moving river?).

Students should develop the habit of stating the goal or goals before they proceed with finding a solution. This serves as a check on problem comprehension and forces the problem solver to consider what sorts of answers are "acceptable." The first stage should also include some estimate of the size of the answer, if at all possible. For example, virtually all students in statistics courses know early in the course that probability values range between 0 and 1, yet many are willing to accept answers that are outside of this range because "that's the way the arithmetic came out."

What Is Known?

This step requires students to consider and explicitly state the information that is given in the problem. Mayer (1986) found that students tend to forget or misrepresent relational aspects of problems (e.g., X is twice Y vs. X is two more than Y), thus it is a good idea to focus directly on the relationships among the variables.

Taken together, the first two steps provide a beginning (the knowns) and end point (goal) for any problem. Virtually all students can have some success with these steps and will be engaging in the problem-solving process.

The recognition of a problem as belonging to a class of problems also facilitates performance. If a problem can be identified as a "work" problem or a "distance" problem, for example, then students can apply appropriate procedures for moving from the start state (the givens) toward the goal. Students should develop the habit of labeling problems by type as they work on them as a way of practicing the identification of problem types. Mayer (1987a) suggested that problems of mixed types should appear in the same assignment or lesson. This forces the problem solver to identify problems with similar underlying principles as belonging to the same type of problem classification.

A common obstacle to generalizing problem-solving skills is the practice of teaching a solution principle, then testing the student's ability to apply that principle without requiring the student to determine the conditions under which the principle is applicable. For example, I teach statistics at a state university. When students are given assignments that require the use of chi-square analysis on one assignment, *t*-tests on another, and analysis of variance on another, they usually have no difficulty. But when all three types of problems are mixed in a single assignment, they have difficulty deciding which is the appropriate procedure for a given type of problem. Unfortunately, real world problems do not come neatly labeled as to problem type. I have had university professors confide in me that they can "do" any standard statistical analysis, but often do not know which to perform. It is clear that this is not a problem limited to undergraduates. This difficulty was recognized by the French mathematician, Jean Dieudonne, who has called mathematics "the art of selective ignorance" because one must know what to ignore in order to determine what to attend to.

In real-world problems, part of the "trick" in specifying what is known is the ability to decide which information is relevant. Most classroom problems provide students with all of the relevant information and no irrelevant information. Thus, students look for ways to use all of the information provided. It is a good idea to give students some unneeded information and/or to ask them what they need to know in order to solve the problem. This is one way to foster a more thoughtful approach to solving problems.

Which Thinking Skill or Skills Will Help Students Reach Their Goals?

A problem is solved when there is no longer a gap between the start state and the goal. There are numerous suggestions in the literature for moving toward a solution (e.g., Bransford & Stein, 1984). In recent research, Schoenfeld (1985) taught college students five strategies for use with mathematical problems. These strategies should generalize to scientific problems as well. Three of these strategies are useful in any context:

1. Draw a diagram, if at all possible.
2. Consider a similar problem with fewer variables.
3. Try to establish subgoals.

The other two strategies are more specific to mathematical problems:

4. Look for patterns. (If there is an integer parameter, look for an inductive argument. Is there an n or other parameter in the problem that takes on an integer value? List the integer parameters in order, and look for a pattern. Go beyond n objects and see what happens when you pass from n to $n + 1$.)

5. Use contradiction or contrapositive when solving proofs. (Contradiction: Assume, for the sake of argument, that the statement you want to make is false. Using this assumption, go on to prove that either one of the given conditions in the problem is false, or that what you wish to prove is true. Contrapositive: Instead of proving the statement "If X is true, then Y is true," you can prove the equivalent statement, "If Y is false, then X is false.")

After only five training sessions practicing these strategies, the students who received this training were performing significantly better than a comparable control group who did not receive training with these general problem-solving skills. (See Schoenfeld, 1985, for additional details.) Of course, a skills approach to solving problems is not a substitute for instruction in a content area. There is no substitute for knowledge in an academic domain. It is, however, a practical addition to *every course* because a skills approach requires students to become actively involved in the process of solving problems and because it makes implicit thinking strategies more explicit and, thus, easier to learn.

Although I believe that the proliferation of problem-solving courses has generally had a beneficial effect, much of the benefit may be attributable to their focus on "how to solve problems" rather than any specific techniques per se. If a problem-solving approach were incorporated into every course at every level in the sciences and mathematics, then specially designed courses in problem solving might not be needed.

Has the Goal Been Reached?

I have taught statistics for over 10 years. I must have asked students if they have checked their work as often as I have said my name. A concern for accuracy is probably the best predictor of success. Does the answer make sense? Is it close in magnitude to the estimate that was made before finding the solution? If not, why not? Was there a problem with the original estimate or with the derived answer or both? What was learned in solving the problem that can be used in other problems?

The habit of monitoring the solution process (e.g., How will a certain procedure or equation help solve the problem?) and verifying the quality of the product are critical elements of critical thinking. Psychologists call the monitoring process metacognition or "knowledge of what one knows and doesn't know." Griffiths (1976) noted the need for metacognitive strategies when he posed the interesting question, "Physics teaching: Does it hinder intellectual development?" (p. 81). He answered this question by noting that the way physics is often taught, with vocabulary drills and reliance on formulas, prevents students from learning how to reason about the issues. Griffiths found that, "In many instances, when a conflict was apparent between the predicted results and the experimental evidence, a technical term was imposed to explain the discrepancy" (p. 84). Here is one of his student's responses to a classical problem involving an inclined plane: "You have to calculate it. You must set all forces to zero, then sum all the forces acting on the body equal to zero, then solve for what it really means" (p.84). You do not need to be a professor of physics to realize that this student is in trouble. He has acquired a meaningless vocabulary and has not acquired the ability to think in a cogent way about topics in physics. More troublesome than the student's lack of knowledge is the fact that he doesn't seem to know that he doesn't know. He has not developed the ability to monitor his knowledge and recognize the difference between scattering terms and understanding concepts. He has no awareness or self-monitoring process for his own knowledge.

Transfer of Training

The most important rule in thinking skills instruction is to teach for transfer, because the ultimate goal of this approach is to develop students who can solve a large variety of novel problems, not just those previously presented in assignments. The ability to transfer skills learned with one set of problems to a different set of problems is what I mean by mathematical and scientific thinking. The little research that exists on the ability to transfer skills suggests that students can learn to think mathematically and scientifically and that they can use this knowledge successfully when they encounter problems that are different from those they previously encountered (Mayer, 1988b; Schoenfeld, 1985). Similarly, Catrambone and Holyoak (1987) found that when students receive explicit training in identifying subgoals in mathematical problems, they perform better on problems that are dissimilar to the ones they learned than a control group of students.

ABSTRACT THINKING SKILLS

The Swiss psychologist Jean Piaget is best known for his studies of the development of abstract thinking skills. According to Piaget, thinking skills develop in qualitatively distinct stages with the highest level of development, *formal operations* or *formal thought*, needed for complex scientific reasoning. When individuals attain this skills level, they can formulate hypotheses (What would happen if . . .) and manipulate abstract symbols such as the ones needed to understand algebra and geometry. Consider the intellectual abilities associated with formal thought:

> Very simply, it is the period in which most of us become able to reason abstractly—to hypothesize and work from the abstract to the particular, instead of the other way round, or even work from the abstract to the abstract. During this period we form and use concepts of proportion (i.e., of a relation between relationships), of law, of justice, of infinity, and so forth. (Sime, 1973, p. 14)

Several researchers (e.g., Collea & Nummedal, 1980) have designed educational programs in which students learn the scientific thinking skills investigated by Piaget. The goal of these programs is to enhance the level of thought each individual is able to attain and to thereby improve students' abilities in mathematics and the sciences.

Consider the following problems:

1. A researcher is interested in finding out how weight, exercise, and heredity affect blood pressure. How can she or he go about determining the influence of these variables?

2. A laboratory task involves mixing colorless chemicals until a yellow color is obtained. If you were given four bottles of chemicals and an activating liquid (which is always needed to obtain the yellow color), how would you go about finding out which chemical combinations will yield a yellow solution?

3. Your shadow is 10 feet long. The shadow of a nearby pole is 25 feet. How tall is the pole?

4. People who take heroin often report that they smoked marijuana when they were teenagers. Can we conclude that smoking marijuana causes people to take heroin?

According to Piaget (Inhelder & Piaget, 1958) the skills needed to solve these problems are characteristic of formal thinking. In order to answer the first question correctly, students must have developed the concept of isolation and control of variables. The second problem requires systematic combination of all chemicals with the activating liquid one at a time, then two at a time, and so on. The third problem requires the ability to reason with proportions. The final problem involves the distinction between correlation and cause. These are general scientific thinking skills that are needed in a wide range of contexts. All of these tasks require the individual to develop an organized approach to the problem—to generate hypotheses and perform all of the appropriate tests.

McKinnon (1976) is one of many advocates for incorporating applications of Piaget's theories into the college curriculum. He administered Piagetian tasks like those presented here to college students at seven institutions. He found that approximately 50% of the college students were not operating at the formal level of thought. In response to the obvious need to teach thinking skills to college science students, McKinnon developed an experimental curriculum that included "all the elements of inquiry—questioning, classifying, hypothesizing, verifying, restructuring, interpreting, and synthesizing" (McKinnon, 1976, p. 118). The success of this course was measured by comparing the number of students who had completed his experimental thinking course and had demonstrated that they were functioning at the formal level of thought with the number of students who scored at this level without taking the course. Many more students from the experimental group (those who took the course) performed at the formal thought level than from the control group (those who took other college courses). There are numerous other demonstrations that certain educational experiences can help students to think at an abstract level (e.g., Chance, 1986; Dansereau et al., 1979; Fox, Marsh, & Crandall, 1983; Herrnstein, Nickerson, de Sanchez, & Swets, 1986; Schoenfeld, 1987a; Wheeler & Dember, 1979). Renner (1976) optimistically concluded that "The research . . . leaves no doubt that intellectual development can be an outcome of education" (p. 190).

USING TECHNOLOGY TO ENHANCE EDUCATION

It may seem superfluous to state to an audience of scientists and mathematicians that there have been radical changes in technology over the last hundred years. Yet, a visitor to almost any classroom in the United States might think he or she wandered into a time warp. College lecture classes, which are the dominant mode of delivery for introductory courses in the sciences and mathematics, look much the same as they did at the turn of the century. Most of the instruction time is spent with a professor speaking and hundreds of students presumably listening and taking notes. Occasionally, a film may be shown, although due to funding restrictions at most universities, the film is likely to be old (students love the crew cuts and bell bottom pants) and not likely to engage student interest. Many of the so-called educational films are celluloid versions of the lone professor.

There are alternatives to the "talking head" model of education. Technology can be harnessed that will have many advantages over traditional modes of instruction. A computer-based program with a modem or other communication device can be used to individualize learning, provide a more active mode of responding, detect errors and gaps in knowledge early in the learning process, and provide the same high quality of learning experiences to students across the entire spectrum of socioeconomic status. The issue of equity is especially important because, as noted earlier, many minorities and females have low participation rates in the sciences and mathematics. If the program includes communication with other students throughout North America, it can foster ethnically, geographically, and economically diverse learning groups. The technology already exists that will allow the possibility of creating an interactive national and international "classroom" via communication networks.

Some types of scientific and mathematical information are best conveyed with video and computer technology. For example, it is more difficult to understand sine waves, rotation in three-dimensional space, and color mixing when they are depicted in static images than when they are shown in moving and colored arrays. Instructional aids that utilize a video monitor allow for a dynamic depiction of change of state information.

I have argued elsewhere for the need to provide more spatial training instruction in school (Halpern, 1986a, 1986b, in press). There is a large research literature showing that, in general, girls score lower on some tests of spatial ability than boys. (See Halpern, 1986a, for a review of the literature.) We also know that spatial ability improves with appropriate instruction (Smith, Frazier, Ward, & Webb, 1983; Sprafkin, Serbin, Denier, & Connor, 1983). Thus, the use of educational technology that enhances the development of spatial skills should be particularly useful for females. Spatial skills are essential for success in many areas of mathematics (e.g., geometry, topology, calculus) and in the sciences (e.g., understanding complex three-dimensional structures).

A technology-based program will present a unique opportunity to study the process of knowledge acquisition in depth. It is possible to design programs that can map knowledge structures for each student by examining error patterns, reaction times, and responses to essay questions. Such programs would allow researchers to investigate variables like the rate of knowledge acquisition and speed and accuracy of retrieval in a more fine-grained way than was ever possible in the past. The information can be used to provide feedback to individual students and can be aggregated so that researchers and educators can understand the learning process better.

Of course, quality educational programs are costly to design and implement, but they have the advantage of widespread use if they are done well and can be cost effective. Quality technologically based programs can also be offered to the general public in a variety of locations like libraries, shopping malls, senior centers, and specially created learning centers where adults and children can use them informally or as part of course work.

One important benefit of improving instruction in the sciences and mathematics will be to make the science and mathematics educator more prestigious and respectable. Too many of our most brilliant scientists and mathematicians still believe that teaching is an activity for those who cannot get research funds. Efforts spent on improving teaching and learning often are unrewarded during the tenure and promotion process. The very language of academics reinforces the negative stereotype of teaching when faculty speak of "teaching loads" and "research opportunities." We cannot have a technologically advanced society without investing in science and mathematics education.

IMPLICATIONS FOR TEACHING AND LEARNING

Four relatively easy changes that should result in improved teaching and learning in mathematics and the sciences can be derived from the cognitive skills approach. They do not require any additional training for current faculty to incorporate into their curriculum, and the changes can be made immediately. They can be summarized as follows:

1. Laboratory and/or class time should be set aside for small group problem-solving sessions. When students are encouraged to work together a number of beneficial practices occur simultaneously. Students remain actively involved in the task. When students are also required to think aloud, they "model" the problem-solving process for each other, with the better students reinforcing and repeating instruction for the weaker students. Group problem solving also provides each student with immediate feedback and identification of difficult areas. The social interaction also increase attachment to the course of study, which has been shown to be a major variable in increasing student retention rates and student satisfaction (Clark & Halpern, 1990).

2. To encourage critical thinking, the problems that students are given to solve must require more than the rote application of a previously learned formula. Problems should be embedded in a real-world context, complete with irrelevant information, and multiple decision points.

3. Students should begin the problem-solving task by diagramming the information and/or writing a summary of the given information and the desired answer. Students will develop the habit of approaching problems this way if the professor requires a systematic approach that uses both spatial and verbal modes of thought. Depending on the context, students should also be required to estimate the size of the answer before they begin to solve the problem and to check the obtained answer with their estimate. If the obtained answer is highly discrepant from the estimated one, students should try to explain why.

At least in the learning stages, every time students apply a formula, they should be required to state or write why they selected that particular formula. This practice will force students to attend to the meaningful components of every problem and see the connection between the components of the formula and the desired answer.

4. Professors need to develop the habit of highlighting transferable skills. For example, if a biology problem requires a distinction between correlation and cause, the generality of this skill should be made explicit along with examples from other academic domains.

The corporate world has long realized the importance of training qualified personnel as the best way to build corporate excellence. Students who comprise the next generation of mathematicians and scientists deserve that as well.

ACKNOWLEDGEMENT

I thank Dr. Robert Stein, Chair of the Mathematics Department at California State Univesity, San Bernardino, for insightful comments on an earlier draft of this manuscript.

2

The *Jasper* Series: An Experiment with New Ways to Enhance Mathematical Thinking

James Van Haneghan
Northern Illinois University

Linda Barron
Vanderbilt University

Michael Young
University of Connecticut

Susan Williams
Nancy Vye
John Bransford
Vanderbilt University

Instruction in mathematical problem solving has been an important focus for cognitive scientists and mathematics educators (e.g., Carpenter & Moser, 1982, 1983; Lesh, 1981; Silver, 1985). Nevertheless, national assessments of children's mathematics achievement still find problem solving to be a weakness of many children (e.g., Fourth National Assessment of Educational Progress in Mathematics; Kouba et al., 1988). Children fail to bring "real-world" standards to their work (Silver, 1986; Van Haneghan & Baker, 1989), have difficulty with two-step word problems and problems that involve reasoning skills (Kouba et al., 1988), and often have difficulties linking mathematical concepts with arithmetic procedures (Hiebert & LeFevre, 1986). Kouba et al. (1988) also reported that children tend to access inappropriate problem schemata or give up when faced with unfamiliar or complex word problems. They report that children tend to either say that there is not enough information to solve the problem or try to apply some simple familiar procedure when faced with something that is the least bit out of the ordinary. For instance, they might add two numbers together when they should have been multiplied, or simply add all the numbers when there are extraneous numbers present (Furman et al., 1989). Given all these difficulties that children have in working with word problems, it is not surprising to find that cartoonist Gary Larson portrayed "Hell's Library" as a collection of volumes of mathematics word problems. For many children, working with word problems is truly an unpleasant experience.

The reasons that children are poor problem solvers are many, and we believe along with others (e.g., Brown, Collins, & Duguid, 1989) that much of the problem has its roots in educational practices that produce "inert," unused knowledge (Whitehead, 1929). In this chapter, we begin by examining these practices and why we believe the knowledge they produce is inert knowledge. Then we describe the beginnings of our research program designed to help middle school children develop their abilities to apply relevant knowledge in everyday problem-solving situations. Our approach focuses on the use of videodisc technology as a tool to present and teach applied problem solving.

THE PROBLEM OF INERT KNOWLEDGE

By inert knowledge, we are referring to knowledge that is potentially applicable to a variety of contexts but is only accessed in a small set of circumstances (Whitehead, 1929). As an illustration, consider the typical problem-solving activity undertaken by middle school children in classrooms—word problems. Typical word problems involve the presentation of two quantities and a question about those quantities. The main problem for children is to select which arithmetic procedure to apply to find the answer. Usually, the operation can be selected by knowing a "key word" that is associated with carrying out a particular operation. Sometimes children will receive two-step problems or problems that have irrelevant or insufficient information, but for the most part the standard word problem is an exercise in figuring out the correct operation to apply. But even this is not necessary when children are presented with a large number of word problems involving the same operation. Porter (1989) noted that in such cases solving word problems is simply additional drill and practice working with the various arithmetic operations.

One reason that the knowledge acquired from such activity becomes inert is that it does not represent an analogue of real-world problem solving. Applied problem solving involves more than simply figuring out which procedure to apply—it involves constructing the question itself and finding the information necessary to solve the problem (Bransford, Hasselbring et al., 1988; Brown et al., 1989; Lesh, 1981; Porter, 1989). The ultimate goal of such problem-solving activity may not even be finding the mathematical answer. For instance, imagine planning a vacation on a budget. Arithmetic is used largely as a means to an end rather than an end in itself. The ultimate goal is to have the best vacation possible within budget constraints. Mathematics is important only to the extent that arithmetic procedures can be used to help achieve the goals defined by the person planning the trip (Lesh, 1981). It is a tool to be used in conjunction with other factors to arrive at a decision about which vacation choices to make. The use of arithmetic to help develop plans of action and make decisions is the way we tend to use mathematics in the everyday world. It is, in Brown et al.'s (1989) terminology, "authentic activity" (p. 34). Such decision making and planning are rarely part of word problems children see in classrooms.

Not only is it the lack of practice in planning and decision making that leads to inert knowledge, it is also the lack of authentic goals in word problems. For example, we recently purchased a set of commercially available problem-solving materials that includes a problem about a trip to a haunted house. The problem focuses on the fact that there are eight spiderwebs downstairs and six upstairs. Directions to the students are to choose the mathematical operation necessary to determine the total number of spiderwebs. This is hardly an authentic goal for someone entering a haunted house.

Given childrens' experiences with typical word problems, it is not surprising that even when problem goals are realistic, children often deal with the situation unrealistically. For instance, Silver (1986) found that children had difficulty dealing with a problem concerning how many buses would be needed to take a large number of students on a field trip. The children often gave answers that required "fractional buses" or left remainders without much thought about what those remaining students would do. Numbed by unrealistic, trivial goals, children often fail to use their knowledge of mathematics to analyze situations that do have realistic goals.

Such examples call into question the assumption of some educators, who believe that children learn to do applied mathematical problem solving from their work with standard word problems. As Porter (1989) noted, the preponderance of evidence suggests that this assumption is wrong. In fact, as DeCorte and Verschaffel (1985) pointed out, children learn to suspend rather than embrace reality when doing word problems and tend to see the activity of word problem solving as a game governed by its own rules, separate from reality. Word problems lack both realistic goals and important activities that are used when solving "authentic" problems. Without considering these aspects of problem-solving activity, one can hardly expect work with word problems to easily transfer to applied problems. Thus, in order to teach authentic problem-solving activity, one needs a new kind of problem that contains the realistic elements of real-world problems.

ANCHORING MATHEMATICAL PROBLEM SOLVING IN REALISTIC CONTEXTS

Anchored Instruction

Our response to the problem of inert knowledge has been to develop problem-solving contexts that enhance learning and transfer. The studies described in this chapter have been guided by several years of research on ways to create conditions that are favorable for learning. We believe that these conditions include the guidance provided by an effective teacher, a rich, realistic, source of information, and a meaningful context for problem solving (Bransford, Sherwood, Kinzer, & Hasselbring, 1985; Sherwood, Kinzer, Hasselbring, & Bransford, 1987). These components are believed to be important to the learning of preschool children who, despite a lack of knowledge and problem-solving strategies, are able to learn very effectively in their real-world environment with the guidance provided by their parents and other mediators. The real-world environment shared by young children and their parents serves as an anchor to which new information can be connected. We have adapted this idealized learning environment for use in the classroom, and call this concept *anchored instruction* (Bransford, Sherwood, Hasselbring, Kinzer, & Williams, 1990; Bransford, Vye, Kinzer, & Risko, 1990; Cognition and Technology Group at Vanderbilt, 1990).

A primary requirement of anchored instruction is that the teacher and student share a rich context to which many types of new information can be linked. Finding a shared context can be difficult in a classroom where the teacher and students often come from different backgrounds. It becomes necessary to create these contexts in the classroom instead of relying on out-of-school experiences.

Real-life contexts have traditionally been used to anchor instruction. Field trips and laboratory experiments are already an established part of traditional instruction. Apprenticeship learning and on-the-job training are other existing methods that rely on real life to anchor instruction. But these methods are not always practical, efficient, or well-structured, and there cannot be many such experiences packed into each school day. We prefer to use a videodisc medium to provide a context that is rich and that allows the teacher to organize and design the learning experience. We refer to these contexts as macrocontexts because they are broad-based and can be worked on over an extended period of time.

Why Videodisc?

One reason we prefer to use a videodisc is that anchored instruction relies on a meaningful context that is realistic and interesting enough to understand and remember, yet rich enough to support an extended period of study. During this extended study, multiple perspectives are taken on the context; thus a single video story may be examined from the perspective of a scientist, a historian, and a mathematician. By relating all these points of view within the same setting, students are able to understand how these disciplines are related to each other (Bransford, Sherwood, & Hasselbring, 1988). Once the concepts are mastered within one context, new contexts may be introduced by linking them to the original anchor. Videodiscs are particularly advantageous for exploring multiple perspectives because there is often a great deal of incidental information embedded in them. The incidental information can become central if examined from another point of view.

In addition to providing us with a stimulus that can be examined from many different points of view, videodisc anchors have several advantages over text-based anchors. One is that students can directly form a rich image or mental model of the problem situation (Johnson-Laird, 1983; McNamara, Miller, & Bransford, in press). Students would have to construct this model if the anchor were text-based. Skill differences in reading ability and background knowledge can therefore affect the quality of models formed by students from text (Bransford, Kinzer, Risko, Rowe, & Vye, 1989).

Another reason for using videodisc anchors is that they allow students to develop important pattern recognition skills; students have the opportunity to practice defining problems and recognizing information that is relevant to the solution of these problems (e.g., Bransford, Franks, Vye, & Sherwood, 1989). It is more difficult to simulate these activities using text because text represents the output of the writer's pattern recognition processes.

Finally, we believe that videodisc anchors are advantageous because of their random-access capabilities (Sherwood et al., 1987). Unlike linear tape where search time is slow, teachers can almost instantly access information on the videodisc to use for discussion. Since one of our goals is to help students explore the same disc from multiple perspectives, it is important that teachers can quickly and easily access information.

Early Studies

Our early studies on the use of videodiscs to recreate semantically rich, shared contexts were conducted using commercially available movies such as *Raiders of the Lost Ark* and *Swiss Family Robinson* (Bransford, Goin, Hasselbring, Kinzer, Sherwood, & Williams, 1988; Johnson, 1987; Sherwood et al., 1987). Movies were chosen because they are very entertaining to watch, widely available, and low in cost. Furthermore, since they do not contain fixed instructional segments, they can be used flexibly for different ages and for a number of different topics. For example, in the studies described here, the same scenes from *Raiders of the Lost Ark* were used as a context for teaching both mathematics and science.

Our initial studies were conducted with college and junior high school students to understand the effects of using movies to create a context for learning (Sherwood et al., 1987). Students were shown a 10-minute segment of the movie *Raiders of the Lost Ark* that depicts Indiana Jones's trip to South America to find a golden idol. Then they were presented with 13 short passages about science concepts normally encountered in high school. In the experimental group, the passages were related to problems that Indiana might have encountered on his trip to South America. For example, one passage contrasted the density of gold and sand, and related this information to a scene in the movie in which Indiana swaps a bag of sand for the golden idol on a weight-sensitive pedestal. The control group read passages with unrelated contexts. In a test of recall, the experimental group was able to remember a significantly greater number of topics than the control group. Probably even more important was the finding that, when given the task of planning for an expedition somewhat similar to Indiana's trip, the students who had learned the science concepts in the video context gave answers that were more specific, more relevant, and more likely to be related to the information that they had read. Since they had seen examples of how and why information from science lessons could be useful for problem solving, students who learned in the video context spontaneously accessed information when it was useful in a different context.

Another study using *Raiders of the Lost Ark* as a context had the following goal: Assume that we are planning a trip to South America and have only the video to study as we plan for our trip (Bransford, Goin et al., 1988). We need to learn about obstacles that we might encounter. For example, how can we discover the width of the pit that Indiana needed to jump? Since the pit is only a few inches wide on the screen it is not helpful to measure the screen. However, it is possible to use the proportional relationship of a known object to the unknown object. In one scene, Indiana is shown jumping the pit. Using videodisc, it is possible to freeze the video and study it. It is apparent that the pit is two Indiana's wide. If Indiana is 6 feet tall, then the pit is 12 feet wide. Using this model a number of problems were generated and taught to fifth and sixth graders who were at least one year behind their peers in mathematics. It was hoped that the video would improve their understanding of the relationships between known and unknown quantities in the problems, help to convey the value of being able to solve this type of problem, and improve their motivation.

Control group students who received instruction on unrelated word problems without video showed very little improvement. Those receiving the instruction anchored in the video context showed a great deal of change, even when the problems were unrelated to the original *Raiders* context. Evidence of spontaneous transfer is illustrated by the following anecdote. One video group student was observed talking to a friend as they walked across the campus. He was saying, "If I'm 4 feet tall and it takes four of me to equal the lamppost, then the lamppost is 16 feet tall" (see Bransford, Goin et al., 1988).

Although studies using commercially available movies provided very positive results, there were limitations to their use. First, it was difficult to find movies having content that was appropriate for use in the classroom. Only a few had stories with naturally occurring problem situations that could be exploited for educational purposes, and it was often necessary to overlay the movie contexts with imagined goals (e.g., "Pretend that Indiana needed to return to South America"). Second, information important to solving problems encountered in movies was not always presented in the video (e.g., "How tall is Indiana Jones?"

or "How far was it from the cave entrance to the river?"). Of course, we could have instructed our teachers to make up data and provide it to the students. Our preference was to have such information embedded in the video so that students would learn to search for and find what they needed to know to achieve particular goals.

We decided to create a videodisc whose plot contained naturally occurring problem situations, and where the facts needed to solve these problems were included so that students could have the opportunity to practice solving them rather than merely watching them being solved. A prototype called *The River Adventure* was designed and filmed on $\frac{1}{2}''$ VHS videotape. In this adventure, a family wins a one-week vacation on a houseboat. All the information necessary to plan for their trip can be calculated from facts in the videodisc. Students can compute the number of people the boat will sleep, the size of the covered dock necessary to dock the boat, the amount of water necessary for drinking and showers, and so on. There are numerous opportunities for generating and solving simple word problems in this context.

We used this videodisc to attempt to improve the performance of mathematics-delayed students on typical mathematics problem-solving tasks (Furman et al., 1989). Our baseline measures of students' work indicated that they performed very poorly on written word problems, having a particularly hard time with problems containing irrelevant information. Think-aloud protocols indicated that the students did not really understand the problems, but tended to find a key word (e.g., "times") and use that to determine the operation. The operation was used on all the numbers in each problem, even if the numbers involved irrelevant information.

Our baseline measures also indicated that both regular and special education students had great difficulty planning for the trip described in the video. Neither group of students spontaneously used mathematics when they thought about problems such as estimating time of arrival or planning the amount of food and water needed. Additionally, they had great difficulty finding information relevant to solving a particular problem.

Special education students received instruction in *The River Adventure* context designed to facilitate their conceptual understanding of the problems. After instruction on two problem types (measurement problems and distance/speed problems), students received a posttest on out-of-context problems. They performed very well on both problem types even when the problems contained irrelevant information (see Furman et al., 1989). This study demonstrated that problem-solving instruction using specially designed video contexts could help students learn to solve mathematics story problems and that the gains transferred to other contexts. Control students who had received traditional instruction and practice on problems of the same type showed relatively little change in their conceptual understanding.

A SPECIALLY DESIGNED SERIES OF VIDEO ANCHORS: *THE ADVENTURES OF JASPER WOODBURY*

By combining knowledge gained from working with both commercially available movies and *The River Adventure* as contexts for mathematics instruction, an interdisciplinary team composed of educators and cognitive and developmental psychologists developed guidelines to be used in the creation of a series of instructional videodiscs, *The Adventures of Jasper Woodbury*.[1] The initial videodisc in this series and its design is the focus of the present chapter.

The Adventures of Jasper Woodbury: Journey to Cedar Creek is a 17-minute, commercial-quality videodisc that provides a real-world context for teaching mathematical problem solving. The design of the videodisc allows students to formulate problems and to generate the kinds of information needed to solve these problems. In the videodisc, a person named Jasper Woodbury takes a river trip to see an old cabin cruiser he is considering purchasing. Jasper and the cruiser's owner, a woman named Sal, test-run the cruiser, after which Jasper decides to purchase the boat. As the boat's running lights are inoperative, Jasper must determine if he can get the boat to his home dock before sunset. Two major questions that form the basis of Jasper's decision are presented at the end of the disc: Does Jasper have enough time to return home before sunset, and is there enough fuel in the boat's gas tank for the return trip? The story indicates that Jasper decides he can get home before sunset. The students have to decide whether his decision was correct and to solve the problems he had to solve in order to make his decision. As they work through the problems, students discover that this seemingly simple decision involves a great deal of thinking.

Design Principles Used to Develop the *Jasper* Series

The *Jasper* videodisc was explicitly created using specific design principles. Some of these principles are characteristic of macrocontexts we studied previously, such as *Raiders* and *The River Adventure*; other design principles are new and are not present in other existing video. The design principles of *Jasper* were selected because they enable teachers to create specific kinds of mathematical problem-solving experiences for students; in other words, *Jasper* was designed to afford certain kinds of instruction. In the following, we describe the major design principles and their functions.

Video-Based Presentation Format. Earlier, we discussed reasons why we prefer videodisc anchors. The *Jasper* series is also videodisc-based.

---

[1]The general design for a problem-solving series was created by our interdisciplinary research team; the *Jasper* story and video was written, produced, and directed by Thomas Sturdevant. Funding was provided by The James S. McDonnell Foundation and Vanderbilt University.

Narrative Format.   A second design principle is the use of a narrative format to present information. One purpose for using a story is to create a meaningful context for problem solving (see also Lipman, 1985; *Voyage of the Mimi*, Bank Street College of Education, 1985). Stories involve a text structure that is relatively well understood by middle-school students (Stein & Glenn, 1979). Using a meaningful structure as the context for presentation of mathematical concepts should enable students to generate more easily a mental model of the situation and thus enable them to devote more of their attention to problem solving.

An equally if not more important reason for using story contexts is that they help students understand the function of the mathematics concepts. Earlier we discussed the importance of situating instruction in authentic contexts (Brown et al., 1989). The *Jasper* story depicts authentic situations where mathematical problem solving is required. By anchoring instruction in this way, we hope to help students develop knowledge structures that are not inert—that are understood as being relevant to a variety of problem-solving situations.

Another key aspect of the story relates to its content. The story was designed to include key concepts contained in many middle school mathematics curricula. The problem types (e.g., rate problems) and computations (e.g., long division with decimals) found in *Jasper* are representative of those found in typical fifth-through seventh-grade mathematics textbooks. In addition, *Jasper* was designed to include concepts from science, history, and literature. For example, *Jasper* contains examples of many simple machines, a topic covered in fifth-grade science. The story also alludes to *Adventures of Huckleberry Finn*, allowing for discussion of literature and history concepts. Our goal was to design the story in a way that provides opportunities to analyze it from multiple perspectives.

Generative Structure.   The *Jasper* story is a well-formed story, with one exception. As with most stories, there is setting information, a slate of characters, an initiating event, and consequent events. The way in which this story differs is that the resolution of the story must be provided by students. (There is a resolution on the disc, but students see it only after attempting to resolve the story themselves.) In the process of reaching a resolution, students must consider a complex set of mathematical information. One reason for having students provide the ending is that we think it is motivating; students seem to like to determine for themselves whether Jasper makes it home. A second reason is that it allows students to engage in generative learning. An important goal of macro-context instruction is to have students become active generators of knowledge rather than passive recipients (Bransford, Goin et al., 1988).

Embedded Data Design.   An especially important design feature of *Jasper* that makes the generation component work is what we have called *embedded data design*. The mathematical problems are not explicitly presented in the video, as for example word problems are presented in textbooks. To illustrate, consider several scenes from *Jasper*. In the first scene, the viewer meets Jasper who is poring over the classified ads in the newspaper. Jasper sees an ad for a cruiser for sale and he decides to go look at it. Next, we see Jasper at his boat dock where he is preparing his small motorboat for a trip to where the cruiser is docked. We see him check his map for the distance between the two docks and we hear the marine radio broadcasting the current temperature, wind velocity, and time of sunset.

The scenes just described contain *embedded data*. That is, unknown to the viewer the scenes contain information that will be relevant to the solution of the problem that Jasper later faces. Jasper's problem is that having bought the cruiser, he must decide if he can drive it home before dark without running out of fuel. He needs to be home before dark because the cruiser's running lights do not work. At this point, the map becomes important for calculating the distance home, and the time of sunset is important for determining the time available for the trip.

The rationale for incidentally presenting or embedding data is to enable students to take part in problem formulation and pattern recognition activities that traditional word problem solving does not allow, but that are characteristic of applied problem solving outside of the classroom. In the *Jasper* series, students are required to **identify problems** to be solved. Thus, in deciding whether Jasper can get home before sunset, students must first identify that they need to know total time for the trip and the time available for the trip. A second activity in *Jasper* is that students have to **formulate solutions** to problems. For example, in deciding whether Jasper can get home before the sun sets, students must articulate that they need to know the current time and the time of sunset in order to calculate the time available for the trip. A third activity is that students must **recognize relevant number facts** from the videodisc that will enable them to perform the calculations necessary for solving the problems that they formulate.

Recent research suggests that problem formulation and pattern recognition training are sorely missing from mathematics instruction in spite of the fact that they represent important and difficult aspects of higher order mathematical thinking (Porter, 1989).

Problem Complexity. The *Jasper* videodisc poses a very complex mathematical problem comprised of more than 15 interrelated steps or subproblems. The complexity of the problem is intentional. As noted earlier, national scores for mathematics achievement in education (Kouba et al., 1988) indicate that students experience great difficulty solving multi-step problems. Our observations suggest that this occurs because students are not routinely provided with the opportunity to engage in this kind of sustained mathematical thinking. Indeed, some have suggested that traditional curricula are training "1-minute" problem solvers (Lester & Garofalo, 1982). The *Jasper* problem is sufficiently complex to require careful planning on the part of students. In addition, unlike traditional word problems, the *Jasper* problem is an authentic example of applied problem solving where goals and a plan of action must be developed and where mathematics functions as a tool for making plans and decisions.

INITIAL STUDIES WITH THE JASPER CONTEXT

The *Jasper* videodisc has been available since October, 1988; our goal in this section of the chapter is to describe some of our initial research with it. We discuss three types of studies: (a) A baseline study of sixth graders' abilities to formulate and solve the problem depicted in *Jasper*; (b) descriptive studies of teachers' uses of *Jasper* in fourth-, fifth-, and sixth-grade classes; and (c) a controlled instructional study that we conducted that assessed transfer on a complex, *Jasper*-like problem formulation and problem-solving task.

A Baseline Study

In this preliminary investigation, we examined middle-school students' abilities to solve the mathematical problems presented in the *Jasper* videodisc. The study was designed to assess how well students identified and solved the overall problem and subordinate problems without receiving instruction in solving these problems. Participants were sixth graders recruited from a class comprised mostly of high-achieving students.

Problem-solving performance was assessed through individual interviews with the students after they had viewed the video one time. To assist in recall during problem solving, students were provided with still pictures summarizing the *Jasper* story. The pictures included all of the data needed to solve the problems.

Three levels of interview questions of increasing specificity with regard to the *Jasper* problems were designed. These levels allowed problem formulation assessment under conditions of increased assistance. At Level I, no assistance was provided in problem formulation. Directions to the student included, "Jasper has decided he can get the boat home before sunset. Do you think he made the right decision? Tell me as much as you can about all the problems he had to think about to make his decision. Solve these problems if you can." At Level II, students were prompted by providing them with the major problems presented in the video: (a) Does Jasper have enough time to get the boat home before sunset? (b) Does Jasper have enough fuel to get home? and (c) Should Jasper be concerned about money for the trip home? If he should be, for what does he need money, and does he have enough money? At Level III, these subproblems were broken down further into simple word problem-like questions. For example,

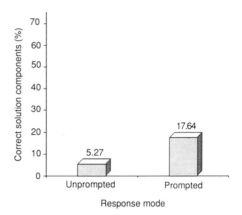

FIG. 2.1   Percent of correct problem formulations at different levels of prompting—baseline study.

students were asked to find the distance from Cedar Creek marina to Jasper's home dock. Students were asked to "think aloud" as they worked and to record their calculations on sheets of paper provided. Interviews were audiotaped.

Transcriptions of the audiotaped interviews and students' written calculations were analyzed with respect to students' problem identification and problem solving. Students' protocols were scored to determine whether the students generated each of the major subproblems, whether they attempted a solution to the problem, and whether their solution was correct.

Students' overall problem-solving performance is summarized in Fig. 2.1. It is clear from the figure that even though the students were high achievers in mathematics, they performed very poorly, regardless of the level of prompting. Less than one-fifth of the students, even when prompted, correctly formulated and solved the problems.

Table 2.1 contains a breakdown of Fig. 2.1. The table indicates the proportion of students who identified and solved the *Jasper* problems at each level of prompting. At Level I, 73% of the students restated the major questions presented at the end of the video, but none of the students included in their discussion Jasper's need to buy gasoline on the way home. Fewer than half of the students attempted to solve the problems they identified, and none of the students completely and accurately solved a major problem. At prompting Level II, a greater proportion of students attempted to solve the problems they identified, but there was only one problem (enough time before sunset) for which a correct solution was produced and only 9% of the students generated correct solutions for this problem. Prompting at Level III resulted in greatly increased attempts to solve the identified problems and greater proportions of students who successfully completed solutions. However, on only one problem (enough gasoline to reach home) did more than half of the students produce correct solutions.

Results indicated that the students were unsuccessful in planning a solution for and solving the macrocontext problems without assistance in problem identi-

TABLE 2.1
Proportion of Sixth-Grade Students Who Formulated Video Problems-Baseline Study

Problem	Level I			Level II			Level III	
	% Mentioning Problem	% Attempting Solution	% Problem Solving	% Mentioning Problem	% Attempting Solution	% Solving Problem	% Attempting Solution	% Solving Problem
Enough time?	73	45	0	NA	91	9	100	0
Enough fuel?	73	36	0	NA	91	0	100	55
Obtain fuel at Willie's								
Enough time?	0	0	0	9	9	0	100	36
Enough fuel	0	0	0	9	0	0	91	45
Buy enough fuel?	0	0	0	91	73	0	100	18

fication. As the prompting became more explicit, more students were able to solve the problems, but problem-solving performance remained poor. Although their problem-solving performance was poor across prompting levels, the students did apply mathematical understandings and skills (at prompting Level III) that they did not access at Levels I and II.

The results of the baseline study were not surprising to us. Students rarely have the opportunity to attempt complex problems like the one in *Jasper* and hence cannot be expected to develop skills of problem formulation and multi-step problem solving. In fact, even college freshmen do very poorly on the *Jasper* problems. Nevertheless, we assumed that fifth- and sixth-grade students could learn to solve problems like the one in *Jasper*. This issue is explored next.

Field Tests of *Jasper*

In order to develop ideas for ways to use *Jasper* in the classroom, we were fortunate to have the opportunity to work with a number of middle-school teachers. The *Jasper* videodisc has been viewed by more than 65 mathematics teachers and science teachers and has been field tested with more than 500 fourth, fifth, sixth, and seventh graders and college students. Teachers who have been introduced to *Jasper* indicated they found the presentation of the material novel and the overall problem challenging. Reviews by middle-school teachers who pilot tested the video in their classes were very positive and indicated that the instructional material was highly motivating to students.

Virtually every teacher who has used *Jasper* noted the videodisc's effectiveness with "nontraditional" learners. According to the teachers, these students who ordinarily contribute little to class discussions did contribute to solving the *Jasper* problem. For example, some of the students noticed information from the video that was relevant for solving the problem. Teachers also mentioned that students exerted a sustained effort in solving the problems posed in the videodisc. One teacher remarked that her fourth graders worked on the problem "for almost an hour and 45 minutes, which is an extremely long time for fourth grade." Students' continuing efforts to solve the problem outside of class was also noted by the teachers. One teacher commented that one of her students, after having seen the video the previous day, said upon entering class, "I kept thinking about that problem when I went to bed last night and right before I went to sleep, I figured out the answer." The teacher added, "They remembered so much from seeing it one day to when they came in the next day. They picked up on all kinds of details."

Students have responded very favorably to their *Jasper* problem-solving experience. Most students have commented on the challenging aspects of the problem. Typical remarks by middle-school students include: "*Jasper* makes us use our brains"; "This is probably harder than anything we've done . . . but yet it's not too hard for us"; and "The problems were kinda hard to figure out. It is real easy when you start but then you need more and more details."

Some of the students found group work useful in solving the *Jasper* problems. One such comment was "I think it was good to work in groups. There may have been one fact that you didn't know that someone else in your group did."

Several students' comments centered on what the video taught the students. One said it taught them to listen. Another said, "It just kinda taught you to use common sense." Another particularly noteworthy comment was "It taught us to use our short-term memory."

In addition to obtaining reactions from educators and students who have used the *Jasper* video, we have observed and videotaped local teachers using the videodisc in their classes.[2] These teachers' instructional practices with the problem-solving video, especially those involving small group work and presentations of problem solutions, contributed to the selection of teaching methods employed with the experimental group in our initial *Jasper* instructional experiment (to be discussed later). The teachers with whom we have worked have been quite receptive to using the videodisc in their lesson presentations. They controlled the disc player with a hand-held remote control device.

A Controlled Instructional Study

The opportunity to observe students and teachers working with *Jasper* was extremely beneficial for us. The experiences convinced us that the problem-solving challenge was motivating to students and that, with teacher guidance and the chance to work in cooperative groups, the students could learn to master the challenge. This provided information for the design of a controlled study that compared the effects on a transfer task of traditional problem-solving instruction with instruction in the context of Jasper.

In our controlled teaching study, instruction in solving the mathematical problems presented in *Jasper* was provided, and effects of this instruction on students' problem formulation and problem-solving abilities were examined. Control students were instructed in unrelated-context problems of the type commonly presented in elementary mathematics textbooks. No video was used in the control condition. The overall goal of the study was to determine if anchored instruction with *Jasper* would produce learning and transfer of learning that was not experi-

[2]We thank Nancy Johnson of Franklin Road Academy, Nashville, TN, Gayle Bagsby, Jenny Harris, Bill Clarkson and Jill Ashworth of Franklin Middle School, Franklin, TN, and Carol Filson of Rose Park Middle School, Nashville, TN, for their assistance in working with the *Jasper* video. We are also grateful to Karen Filippone, fifth-grade teacher from Decatur, GA, for her review of and thoughtful comments regarding the *Jasper* video and to her students, who spontaneously wrote letters giving their reactions to the *Jasper* problem-solving experience. Some of the students' comments are included in this section.

enced by students instructed in word problem solving as presented in a traditional curriculum.

Participants were a fifth-grade class of above-average students. Based on students' scores on the mathematics section of the Stanford Achievement Test, a stratified random assignment was made of students to experimental- or control-group teaching conditions.

The first day of the experiment, the *Jasper* video was shown to all students and then students were pretested. After pretesting, experimental and control students were separated to begin teaching sessions, that were continued for three additional class sessions. Following instruction, students received posttests and were interviewed.

Instruction for Experimental Group.   Students in the experimental group investigated the major questions *Jasper* had to answer. As each question (time, fuel, and money) was introduced in class, students were encouraged to generate subordinate questions of the stated question and to recall relevant facts from the video to answer the questions. This segment of instruction was designed to engage students in planning for problem solving and to focus their attention on gathering the needed information. Students were guided to generate complete solutions for all of the subproblems identified. Conversely, as subproblem solutions were generated, students were encouraged to relate the solutions to the overall problem. Students engaged in problem solving as a class, in small groups, and on an individual basis.

Experimental-group instruction was supported each day by use of videodisc/computer technology. The instructor controlled the disc player by a computer menu prepared prior to the experiment.[3] In addition to the initial showing of *Jasper*, segments of the video were used to help focus students' attention on the overall goals to be achieved. Also, student problem-solving efforts were supported by presentations of video segments containing all of the relevant and some irrelevant data relating to the problem being reviewed. The purpose of this instructional strategy was to engage students in fact finding that required noticing visually- and auditorily-presented information and separating relevant from irrelevant data. The random-access capability of the videodisc allowed the instructor to replay segments students requested to assist them in their problem solving.

Control-Group Instruction.   As mentioned earlier, control students viewed the *Jasper* video along with experimental students the first day of the experiment. Control students, however, received no instruction in solving the *Jasper* problems per se. Traditional teaching methods—teacher lecture, question and answer, worksheets, and teacher and student presentations at the chalkboard—were used to instruct control students in solving traditional word problems. The problems involved distance, elapsed time, rates, fuel consumption, and money, topics

---

[3]This software, Vanderbilt Vision-Maker, was authored by Susan Williams.

around which the overall problem in *Jasper* was structured. The following example typifies problems solved by control students:

> Bill's car averages 25 miles per gallon of gas. At that rate, how many gallons of gas will Bill need to drive 480 miles?

Control students also studied Polya's (1957) problem-solving model and were encouraged to apply the model during problem solving.

Approximately half of the class time was devoted to developing the concepts or procedures to be learned. During the remaining class time, students worked independently or in small groups on worksheets.

Results and Discussion.   A pretest and two posttests were administered to experimental and control students. One of the posttests consisted of unrelated-context word problems. This measure allowed comparison of performance of experimental students to that of control students who were instructed in solving these more routine problems. Somewhat surprisingly, experimental students were able to solve these problems as well as control students despite the fact that the control group had much more explicit practice on these types of problems. Both groups performed quite well on this measure, averaging 77% correct.

A paper and pencil pretest and an identical posttest were designed to assess how well students organized information in the *Jasper* video for problem solving before and after instruction. Students were asked to match factual information needed for solving *Jasper*'s central problems with the appropriate problem. For example, the amount of money Jasper had left would be relevant to the problem of purchasing fuel needed to make the trip home. Experimental students showed significant gains from pretest to posttest whereas control students showed no significant improvement.

The most dramatic finding involved student performance on a video near-transfer postinstruction task. This measure was designed to allow assessment of students' abilities to identify, define, and solve problems similar to those posed in *Jasper*. Performance data were collected in individual interviews with the children. Two levels of prompting were provided. These levels corresponded to Levels I and II described earlier for the baseline study. Students received no assistance in problem formulation at Level I. Level II questions supplied the student with the main problems the video transfer task involved. At each level, students were asked to solve the problems. As was the case in the baseline study, students thought aloud as they worked, and the interviews were audiotaped.

Scores assigned to the interview protocols reflected the completeness and accuracy of the students' problem solutions at each level of prompting. Figure 2.2 contains a summary of students' problem-solving performance on the transfer task. At each level of prompting, protocol scores of students in the experimental group were significantly higher than those of control students. It is evident that, following four sessions of instruction with *Jasper*, experimental students showed

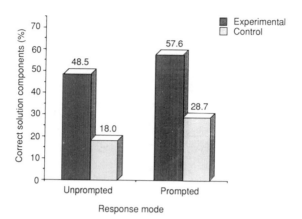

FIG. 2.2   Percent of correct problem formulations at different levels of prompting—transfer study.

significant transfer of learning to a new, similarly complex problem compared to the control students. Several of the experimental students' scores were in the 75–100% range. The maximum control student score was 51%. These results are quite different from those obtained in the baseline study involving students who received no problem-solving instruction.

Experimental students showed great strength in identifying and solving the central distance-rate-time and fuel problems involved in the transfer video. Most of their difficulties seemed to stem from not considering carefully the subordinate problems relating to buying gasoline on the return trip. Several of the students appeared to assume that the character in the transfer story could "somehow" obtain the gasoline on the way home. Although most of the experimental students correctly determined the amount of money left after expenses, few related the result to decisions that needed to be made regarding quantity of gasoline that could be bought on the return trip.

Control students were generally unsuccessful in formulating and solving the video-based transfer problems. Control students, like experimental students, had particular difficulty with decision making relative to the problem of buying gasoline on the way home. One difficulty evident in control students' protocols that was not shown in the protocols of experimental students involved units of measurement. Some control students mixed units (e.g., added hours and miles) and seemed to make little distinction in rates (e.g., minutes per mile and miles per minute). This finding suggests that one benefit of the instruction anchored in the video context may have been clarification of units of measurement.

Our initial attempt to test how well instruction within the *Jasper* context facilitates students' abilities to learn is preliminary. In the future we plan to investigate additional variables such as the effects of different kinds of instruction in a *Jasper* context. Nevertheless, to really assess the power of *Jasper*-like problem-solving environments, we will also need more than one videodisc. We discuss this issue next.

THE IMPORTANCE OF A SERIES

The *Jasper* video previously discussed is considered to be the first in a series of 6 to 10 episodes. The series will focus on the application of middle-school pre-algebra concepts to realistic problems presented in context. Each video will use the central design concepts discussed earlier to help students develop their thinking and problem-solving skills. But no single episode can develop these skills by itself. The series will be designed to provide transfer experiences so that students can focus on the key elements of each video that lead to generalizable mathematics skills.

A letter from a fifth-grade student using the *Jasper* video illustrates the need to emphasize factors that promote transfer. The student wrote that he really liked Jasper but also added: "Next time you make a movie make it on cars 'cause I don't think I'm going to buy a boat when I grow up." For this student, the central theme of the video was the mathematical complexities of buying a boat, rather than the intended theme of how to plan for situations that involve information about speed, time, and distance. The addition of a transfer video designed to explicitly demonstrate the generality of speed-time-distance solutions, to airplanes and hiking for example, would clarify this central theme for the student. Through a series of videodiscs across various contexts, the theme could be further developed and consolidated.

We noted earlier that our current goal is to create a series of 6 to 10 *Jasper* discs that can provide a foundation for using key mathematics concepts in a variety of realistic settings. The second disc in the series has been available since Fall 1989. It involves planning an ultra-light airplane flight to save a wounded eagle. Students must determine the fastest way to get to the eagle and transport it to a veterinarian without running out of gasoline and without exceeding the weight limitations on ultra-lights. The problems to be formulated and solved are similar to the basic problem in the first *Jasper* videodisc; this allows students to discuss the analogies between the first and second episode and experience the fact that it becomes much easier to solve these types of problems the second time around. The second episode includes a number of added twists as well.

We are creating additional discs for the series by working with experts in a variety of areas (mathematicians, scientists,[4] cognitive scientists, students) to

---

[4]We are experimenting with the use of the video design features used in the *Jasper* series to create new material where the major problems involve scientific concepts. A short 5-minute prototype video called *The Golden Statuette* has recently been completed. In order to explain the events in the video, students must apply concepts of displacement and density. Informal studies suggest that the video is motivating but formal research is needed. We would like to have people try it and give us feedback. To receive a copy send $10 to cover shipping and copying to Faapio Po'e, Box 45, Peabody College, Vanderbilt University, Nashville, TN 37203.

find the concepts that they feel are most important. As part of this effort, we have constituted a National Advisory Committee that will advise us. Additionally, we are using the National Council of Teachers of Mathematics (1989) guidelines to help guide our choices of mathematical concepts to include.

We are also creating databases to accompany the *Jasper* videodiscs. We envision these databases as representing a shared body of knowledge, constructed primarily through student research on topics of interest to them. The process of students creating databases around video anchors makes it easier for teachers to introduce mathematics across the curriculum. For example, after experiencing the *Jasper* river adventure, students might research river travel in the era of Huck Finn and recompute Jasper's travel times using speeds appropriate to that era. In science, students might compute motor boat and manatee swimming speeds to consider the impact of motor boat traffic on the survival of the manatee in Florida. These topics, in history and science specifically, suggest ways that mathematics might be integrated across the middle school curriculum through the development of a series of databases.

An important goal for our database extensions is to provide an opportunity for students to experience the distributed nature of intelligence (Pea, 1988). Although traditionally viewed as the fixed property of an individual, intelligence can also be viewed as being distributed across people, places, and even stored in objects such as books, notes, and computers. When viewed in this way, knowledge includes more than facts. Intelligence now includes information about how to access and retrieve knowledge as well as when and how to rely on these alternative sources of information.

A videodisc anchor that would allow students to experience the value of distributing intelligence across the environment would place students in a situation where they were required to make the same types of calculations (or decisions) many times. Students would then be challenged to discover when to use calculators, construct tables, or write computer programs to help with the problems. Of course, in the process they would also learn how to construct and utilize these external sources of knowledge and intelligence.

OUR VISION OF THE FUTURE

Now consider a classroom in the future that incorporates these ideas on ways to use *Jasper* in the classroom. Students have viewed a video that features a charter pilot who must plan departure and arrival times to any location each time a customer comes in. Ten customers have stopped by just in the one day shown. In groups and individually the students have solved several of the mathematics problems using calculators, but decide that a more general computer program is required. They divide the programming task among the groups and proceed to produce their modular travel-time program. Having generated a correct solution to the central problem, the students are asked to view the video in a different way. They are asked to generate all the examples of rates or proportions that were shown in the video or involved in the solution of the problem. Having understood the video in *mathematical* terms, the students are then challenged to re-view the story and take the perspective of a *scientist* interested in all the possible examples of simple machines that were shown. Then after experiencing the video from a mathematic and a scientific perspective, the students are again asked to view the video with a *historical* perspective, comparing the problem shown in the video to that shown in the story of the Spirit of St. Louis, for example.

The students have generated ideas and researched various topics of interest. They organize and write their findings from these various perspectives that incorporate their own unique backgrounds and that of their school and community. They enter their ideas and the associated illustrating video segments into a computer database, which is then challenged by a science class from across the state. The challenging class identifies all the examples of simple machines that they can, and checks the existing database to see if all are included. The same is done in mathematics and history and new contributions that result are added to the database and are immediately shared nationwide by electronic mail. The different cultures, schools, and communities of the participating students lead to new and varied insights and to a database of shared knowledge beyond the capabilities of any individual participant or school. This is not a vision of the future that is far away. The computer, telecommunications, and interactive videodisc technology currently exist.

The preceding example highlights a number of key ideas that will continue to be the focus of our research. First, the students view a single macrocontext from multiple perspectives, specifically those of a mathematician, scientist, and historian. Second, students are given the opportunity to practice taking and understanding multiple perspectives on the same problem or set of issues. Third, students are able to work collaboratively to generate knowledge and share that knowledge through the use of telecommunications. And fourth, interactive video provides an anchor for challenging students across subject areas.

IMPLEMENTATION OF THE *JASPER* SERIES

Anyone with experience in educational settings realizes that programs such as *Jasper* cannot be viewed as stand-alone entities. In order to be effective the *Jasper* series requires excellent teaching, which in turn requires that *Jasper* fit with the curricular goals of particular school systems. We are attempting to work with teachers in order to find the kinds of support needed to implement the series satisfactorily. Some of the basic points we considered—and pitfalls we are trying to avoid—are discussed in the following.

Working in a Variety of Classrooms
With a Variety of Constraints

One of the major pitfalls that plagues curriculum developers stems from their failure to realize that their curricula involve more than the materials themselves. Pilot tests of curricula often rely on the expertise and teaching skills of the developers and their staffs. In addition, developers often use highly motivated (often very high achieving) students, and tests of the curricula often take place under ideal circumstances for implementation (e.g., few time or financial constraints).

We have been attempting in our work to be very sensitive to realistic constraints on the implementation of *Jasper*. First, we have included "front line" teachers in the development of the *Jasper* series. We have been studying intact classes in the context of real schools to assess time, equipment, and financial constraints that could affect adoption and implementation. Second, we have been working to find ways to use the series with and without large amounts of technological or financial investment. For example, a videotape player or a videodisc player and a hand-held remote can be used by someone who does not have the finances to purchase a computer to interface with the videodisc player. Third, we have been working on ways to make the financing and technological expertise available to teachers. In a project led by the Chancellor at Vanderbilt (Joe B. Wyatt), we are engaged in a corporate sponsorship plan to help make implementation a reality without overburdening already financially strapped school systems. Along with financial support, corporations can also offer technological support to schools. Indeed, part of Chancellor Wyatt's plan includes the corporation "lending" the school an individual to help set up and put in place the technology needed to implement *Jasper* and other technology-based curriculum. Many corporations, faced with concerns that the educational system is not adequately training students to participate effectively in the work force, view investment in curricula like the Jasper series as worthwhile venture (e.g., see Kuhn, 1990). Thanks to their efforts, we will be able to assess the implementations of *Jasper* in a variety of settings and states.

Providing Necessary Training

A second pitfall faced by many curriculum developers is their failure to adequately train and provide support to teachers when the curriculum becomes widespread. We are carrying out several kinds of activities to help us avoid this trap. First, we are doing extensive research on how to best train teachers before we formally spread the curricula nationwide. For example, we are holding two intensive workshops on the *Jasper* series so that we may evaluate the effects. Second, we are integrating the use of videodiscs into our preservice courses for teachers. We are hoping that the teachers we train and those trained by other universities will become sufficiently fluent in the technology and curricula behind *Jasper* so that they will be able to easily implement it in schools and perhaps do some training of their colleagues. Third, we are developing training videos to help teachers actually see rather than just read about how to teach with *Jasper*. Fourth, we hope to set up an electronic-mail address (e-mail) or phone "hotline" for teachers to contact us when they have problems or new ideas.

Integrating the Series
With Existing Curricular Goals

A third challenge that is faced by curriculum developers involves the challenge of creating a program that can be integrated with curricular goals of particular schools and teachers. In our ongoing work with teachers we are attempting to do this in a variety of ways. First, by working with teachers in different schools, we are getting a sense of the diversity of goals. Second, we are experimenting with different formats (print, computer-based) that will allow teachers to link specific goals with the *Jasper* curricula. For example, all teachers teach problem solving in the fifth grade and *Jasper* fits that goal well. But how about more specific goals such as learning about decimals and fractions, learning about units of measurement such as inches, feet, miles, and so forth? We are currently working with teachers to use scenes from the *Jasper* series to help them teach specific concepts (e.g., teachers might ask whether the little boat in *Jasper* is 14 inches, feet, or miles long; or whether 4.8 gallons of gas is closer to 4 or 5 gallons). We are also experimenting with ways to make it easy for teachers to link goals with specific questions and *Jasper* scenes.

Creating Informative Assessments

A fourth potential barrier to widespread adoption involves the development of adequate assessment tools. If teachers cannot adequately see what children have learned, they are likely to feel that the students may be wasting their time. In addition, consistent assessments can help assure us that children are learning what we want them to learn from the curricula. We are working to develop assessments that are sensitive to what the curriculum provides, but can be administered within the context of the classroom. Additionally, we are creating a database of assessment tools that we and teachers have developed to help give users of the curricula a choice in how they evaluate it. The database will be dynamic in that the teachers can contribute new assessment tools and the results of assessment research can be used to update it from time to time. Our overall goal for assessment is to strive for systemic validity (Frederiksen & Collins, 1989). That is, we wish as much as possible to test the actual skill we are interested in (e.g., complex problem solving), rather than using multiple choice analogues that often lead to teaching to the test rather than the skill.

Providing Mechanisms for a Growing Curriculum

A common pitfall that developers of new curricula make is to assume that curricula are developed in a top down manner. Curriculum developers often dictate to teachers what they should and should not do, giving them little feedback or say in the process of curriculum development. Even though we have some clearly designed purposes for *Jasper*, we developed it with teacher input and more importantly, want to continue to encourage teacher innovation in the context of *Jasper*. It has been our experience that teachers who feel a sense of ownership about a curriculum take it more seriously and use it in innovative and exciting ways. The idea of a database of assessment tools plus an e-mail network that teachers can use to discuss *Jasper* or other issues signals to the teachers that they have a role in its development.

EPILOGUE

These goals for implementation and our goals for research and practice define an ambitious agenda. We have already begun to carry out this agenda in the hope of providing students with experiences that are motivating and will engender the kinds of mathematical and scientific thinking that are needed for the 21st century. We appreciate any help and advice the readers of this chapter are willing to supply.

ACKNOWLEDGMENTS

The research reported here was supported by Grant No. 87–39 from the James S. McDonnell Foundation and Grant No. G008730072 from the U. S. Department of Education. We wish to thank other members of the Learning Technology Center; especially Tom Sturdevant, Laura Goin, Bob Sherwood, Vicki Risko, Chuck Kinzer, Susan R. Goldman, James Pellegrino, and Ted Hasselbring for their contributions to the work reported here.

3

Mathematical and Scientific Thinking in Classrooms and Other Situations

James G. Greeno
Stanford University and the
Institute for Research on Learning

There is widespread agreement that students do less scientific and mathematical thinking than we wish they would. There are, however, two quite different views about the relation of thinking to classroom learning in mathematics and science, which I will call "Thinking with the basics" and "Thinking is basic." According to "Thinking with the basics," the job of classroom learning is to provide basic scientific or mathematical knowledge that students can then use in thinking mathematically or scientifically after they have learned enough and if they are sufficiently talented and motivated. According to "Thinking is basic," learning to think scientifically and mathematically should be a major focus of classroom activity from the beginning.

"Thinking with the basics" says that the infrequency of scientific and mathematical thinking results from something that is wrong with students. They lack the special talent or motivation that is needed or they have not been trained in the general skills of thinking. "Thinking is basic," on the other hand, says that thinking is natural human activity, and the lack of mathematical and scientific thinking by students is not caused by the students, but rather is caused by characteristics of classroom situations that do not support the kind of thinking that we would like.

The two views differ in assumptions that they presuppose about the relation of knowledge and thinking. "Thinking with the basics" presupposes quite a sharp distinction between knowledge and thinking, with the possibility of acquiring a great deal of knowledge without much ability to think, but not conversely. Thinking, on this view, is analogous to a manufacturing process in which knowledge is analogous to the raw materials and energy sources, and ideas, understandings, solutions to problems, and the like are analogous to the manufactured products. If you view thinking as a kind of manufacturing, you will naturally expect that it is important to have a good stock of materials in the form needed for the manufacturing process (e.g., finished steel rather than iron ore, coke or refined gasoline rather than coal or crude oil), and that it would be fruitless to try to encourage students to think before they had acquired a suitable inventory of knowledge.

"Thinking is basic," on the other hand, considers ability to think as a natural human endowment, along with other abilities such as locomotion and communication. A natural endowment does not remove the need for learning or the possibility of large variations in talent or acquired ability. Almost everyone will learn to make very subtle movement patterns in maneuvering through complex environments with obstacles such as crowded city sidewalks, although few will become accomplished ballet dancers or set Olympic records in running the high hurdles. Almost everyone will learn to participate in complex and subtle patterns of conversation with other people in their cultural communities, although few will become Nobel laureates in literature or spell-binding orators.

If we view the ability to think as a natural endowment, we will expect that its growth will depend mainly on opportunities to think. The ability grows through a progression of activities that increase in their difficulty, but they involve thinking from the beginning, rather than having the opportunity to think withheld until an inventory of alleged materials for thinking has been stockpiled. According to this view, we should try to change education in science and mathematics so that mathematical and scientific thinking are the main focus of activities in situations of learning, enabling students to develop their capabilities of scientific and mathematical thinking through elaboration, refinement, and modification of capabilities that they bring.

A VIEW OF MATHEMATICAL
AND SCIENTIFIC THINKING

Many people who might agree that children have significant abilities for ordinary thinking would doubt that they have significant abilities for thinking mathematically or scientifically unless they receive special educational training. A discussion of this question presupposes at least a general view of what scientific and mathematical thinking are.

The question of mathematical and scientific thinking is a theoretical problem for cognitive science. Therefore, what I offer here as a view that underlies my discussion should be taken as a hypothesis, albeit a broad hypothesis. Although the view that I propose is too general to allow for a direct empirical test, it is certainly subject to revision in the light of scientific research of a kind that many cognitive scientists are conducting (see, e.g., Gardner et al., 1990).

I propose that we take mathematical thinking and scientific thinking to be activities in which concepts and methods of a mathematical or scientific discipline are used in understanding, including understanding involved in solving a problem. The thing that is understood may be a concept or problem within the discipline or something outside the discipline whose understanding is informed by the discipline's resources. This view denies that there is mathematical thinking apart from the concepts and methods of mathematics, or that there is scientific thinking apart from the concepts and methods of the various sciences. Indeed, on this view it is more appropriate to talk about thinking within the various fields of science, biological thinking, chemical thinking, physical thinking, cognitive-scientific thinking, and so on, than it is to talk about scientific thinking in general, although there are some significant aspects of thinking that are shared across the scientific disciplines. Even so, I argue that significant mathematical and scientific thinking is done by children, and that the task of school learning should primarily be to strengthen and refine these capabilities, rather than primarily providing knowledge of terms and procedures that are thought to be the materials on which thinking has to be based.

Many important features of mathematical or scientific thinking are seen in a person's ability to participate in mathematical or scientific discourse. The disciplines of mathematics and science have characteristic forms of discourse, including ways of formulating conjectures and claims and ways of supporting conclusions. The functions of discourse are crucial in the intellectual practices of a discipline, and support the characteristic ways in which the concepts and principles of the discipline are advanced and used in facilitating understanding. As Pea and Greeno (1990) have argued, learning to participate in the discourse forms of the discipline can be viewed as a significant aspect of learning in the discipline—perhaps the most important aspect of learning that is available publicly for evaluation of a learner's progress.

If we want students to learn to participate in mathematical and scientific discourse, there is an implication that seems obvious: Classroom activities should be organized as mathematical or scientific discourses that students can learn to participate in. Normally, the discourse in classrooms is very one-sided: Teachers present information and ask questions; students listen and take notes and answer questions when they are called on. Students may be encouraged to ask questions when they do not understand something that the teacher has said. Students, however, usually are not expected to contribute substantively to the conversation.

A very different kind of discourse is needed if we adopt the view that classroom experience should enable students to participate in mathematical and scientific discourse that involves significant thinking. The conversations need to be of a kind that students can contribute to on the basis of their current understanding, and that will result in stronger understanding by the students, including stronger capabilities of participating in the discourse. On this view—one aspect of the view that "Thinking is basic"—classroom activities should be organized as conversations in which students propose their understandings of a question, discuss each others' views and the assumptions that underlie alternative opinions, and work to resolve different opinions and to reach mutual understanding of scientific or mathematical concepts and other matters that are informed by mathematics or science.

In order for classrooms to be productive forums for mathematical and scientific discourse, students need significant capabilities for thinking mathematically and scientifically. Whether students have such capabilities is a question of fact, and considerable evidence favors a positive assessment of students' capabilities for scientific and mathematical thinking. In this chapter I discuss some of that evidence, mainly in the domain of mathematics. The evidence is in the form of showing circumstances in which significant mathematical thinking by students and other young people occurs. The argument has three main parts, concerning conceptual competence, everyday quantitative reasoning, and demonstrations of classroom practice.

COMPETENCE FOR PARTICIPATING
IN SCIENTIFIC AND MATHEMATICAL DISCOURSE

There is an obvious objection to the proposal that classrooms should become forums of mathematical and scientific conversations. If someone believes in "Thinking with the basics," he or she will object immediately that students cannot participate in scientific or mathematical conversations until they have been taught the basic material of scientific and mathematical knowledge that the conversations should be about. "Thinking is basic" presupposes that students start with sufficient understanding to engage in significant conversations that they can learn in and contribute to.

A growing body of research findings is providing evidence that children understand many concepts and principles implicitly before they receive instruction that enables them to define the concepts or state the principles explicitly. There have been studies of this kind in several conceptual domains, including concepts about life and animacy (Carey, 1985), concepts of causality (Bullock, Gelman, & Baillergeon, 1982), concepts about the mind (Wellman & Estes, 1986), and concepts of number (Gelman & Gallistel, 1978; Gelman & Greeno, 1989; Gelman & Meck, 1986).

I illustrate research of this kind with an example from my laboratory. My collaborators in this research include Joyce L. Moore, Richard Mander, Jan Kerkhoven, and Margaret Korpi. Greeno and Moore (1990) presented a more complete report of this study. The research is about the concept of function. It is widely believed that students do not come to understand this concept very well, even when they have studied high school algebra, and there is evidence that supports this belief (Dreyfus, 1983; Greeno et al., 1985; Janvier, 1978; Schoen-

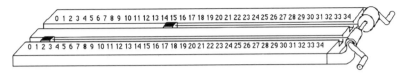

FIG. 3.1.   A pair of winches.

feld, Arcavi, & Smith, in press; Wagner & Kieran, 1989). In the standard curriculum, the concept of function is defined, students are given symbolic problems involving solutions of equations, and they are given word problems that use the equations. Little in the way of mathematical thinking about functions occurs.

We are conducting research using the simple machine shown in Fig. 3.1, adapted from a device used by Piaget, Grize, Szeminska, and Bang (1968/1977). This apparatus is a wooden board about a yard long, with two straight grooves. Each groove has a small metal block with a pointer—one pointer is red, the other is blue. Each block has a string tied to it. The other end of each string is connected to a spool on an axle that can be turned with a handle. There are different spools varying in circumference. The two axles can be turned independently, or they can be linked together so that turning one spool turns the other as well. We have conversations with students about where the blocks will be after the handles are turned: For example, if the block that starts behind has a larger spool, how many turns will be made before the blocks are at the same location.

Another apparatus that we use is a set of rectangular clear plastic tanks, all 1 inch deep and varying in width (and therefore cross-sectional area). The tanks are marked with lines 1 inch apart. One example setup is in Fig. 3.2. The lines on one vertical pair of tanks are red, and the lines on the other vertical pair of tanks are blue. Water is placed in the upper tanks at the level marked 0. Water may or may not be placed in the lower tanks. The discussion is about what happens if water is drained from the upper tanks into the lower tanks, going down to specified levels in the upper tanks or going up to specified levels in the lower tanks. Comparisons can be made, for example: If water is drained from both top tanks down to 5, how much higher will the level be in the blue bottom tank than in the red bottom tank?

Each winch and each vertical pair of tanks embodies a linear function. The mathematics of these systems can be expressed easily as equations of the form $y = mx + b$. For a winch, y is where the block is after the handle is turned, m is the circumference of the spool, x is the number of turns, and b is the position where the block starts. For a pair of tanks, y is the level in the bottom tank after some water is drained, m is the ratio of the size of the top tank to the size of the bottom tank, x is the number of inches drained from the top, and b is the level in the bottom tank initially. Conversations about one track of the winch or one pair of tanks are concerned with a single linear function. Conversations about rela-

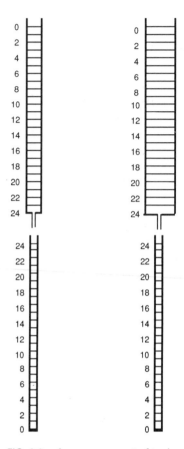

FIG. 3.2.   An arrangement of tanks.

tions between the two tracks or between two vertical pairs of tanks are concerned with a pair of related functions.

In research, we are investigating students' capabilities of thinking about the functional relations among quantities in these situations. To the extent that they can reason about the relations between quantities, students understand the linear functions that relate the quantities, at least implicitly. We have interviewed students in the 7th, 9th, and 11th grades using the winches, and in the 7th and 9th grades using the tanks. Our interviews are conducted with pairs of students, either both girls or both boys. We ask the students' mathematics teachers to recommend pairs of students whom they judge to be at about the national average in mathematics achievement, and who are friends.

The interviews that we conducted were about 45 minutes long. For the first 15–20 minutes, students became familiar with the machine. The interviewer set up different situations involving both tracks and students answered some questions that were quite open-ended. In a second section, the students solved problems in which the interviewer specified some outcomes involving both tracks or two pairs of tanks and the students were asked how they could be made to happen. Third, situations were set up and students were asked to make relatively specific inferences about quantitative properties. We interviewed 8 pairs of students who were in 7th grade and had studied no algebra, 11 pairs of students who were in 9th grade and were near the end of their first year of algebra, and 4 pairs who were in 11th grade and were near the end of their second year of algebra.

To illustrate the reasoning that students exhibit, here is a transcription of part of a conversation by two 7th-graders. The students were working with the winches, and the question was, "How can you make both blocks get to 24 at the same time?" The pair's initial solution was to use the same spool size for both tracks and start both blocks at zero, and they had confirmed their solution using 6-spools. (Every pair of students gave an initial solution with equal values of all three variables.) Then the interviewer asked, "What if you wanted to use different spools and still wanted to have them get to 24 at the same time?" The conversation proceeded as follows:

[Example 1, W7.3]
    S1: Put maybe the blue one or a red one ahead of them, ahead of—
    S2: Or you could just put two different numbers that went to 24—
    S1: —like a 4 or a 6—
    S2: —on each one, and we joined these up, and turn them at the same, well if they're joined up they'll turn around at the same sort of rate, and then, um, it'll reach it.
  INT: Okay, you want to try that?
    S2: Yeah.
  INT: It's easiest if we just pull these back to the beginning, and then you, and then the strings come off real easy. [Place both blocks at 0.] Okay.
[S1 and S2 change spools.]
    S2: Which, what are you using?
    S1: I am using the 4; try the 3.
  INT: OK, where are you going to start?
[S1 and S2 pull the blocks to 0 and check the spools.]
    S1: What do you have, a 2?
    S2: I have a 3.
    S1: You have a 3?
    S2: Yeah, I have a 3.
    S1: Oh, okay, and I have a 4.
  INT: Right.
    S1: So wait, you need to start—for every—you need to start on 3 ahead. [Turns handle until S2's block moves 1 in.] Ok, wait a minute, start here—and it will be 4, then 2, 8, 3 [continues to turn the handle for S2's block]. Let's see—
    S2: —3—

S1: Ok, here we go, I've got it, kind of.

INT: Okay.

S2: Mine needs 8 turns to get to 24.

S1: [marking distances on ruler with fingers] So, what you need to set yours—2 ahead, so 6.

S2: Mine needs 8 and yours takes—

S1: You need to start yours there—[turns handle]—I think there.

S2: Mine needs 8 and yours needs 6—

S1: Yeah, and then you have to be 6 ahead.

S2: Yeah.

S1: 8 or 6, what do you think? Let's try 6.

S2: Yeah.

S1: Let's try it. [Both students start turning handles that are not linked.] Oh, wait, it's not hooked.

INT: So you want these—[reposition blocks at 0 and 6].

S2: Yeah, get mine at 6.

INT: Ok, this one's at 0 and this one's at 6, and we're gonna see what happens. [S1 turns handle.] Yeah, it kind of jumps a little. Pretty close, I think this is about as close as it gets. Okay, you want to say anything more—you felt as though you had to try it, right? You weren't absolutely sure it was gonna work.

S2: No, we weren't definite.

INT: But you made a good, a good prediction.

S1: Yeah.

INT: Can you say any more about how you were, about why you weren't sure—or can you think of a way you would have known for sure?

S1: Well, testing, you can always tell.

INT: Well, that's true.

S2: We have to work out how many times, the rotations and the different numbers. And you have to work out his number of rotations to mine and then you have to set the one, which whatever, forward, and you have to work it out, I found it hard working out how many spaces forward you have to set it—

INT: Uh huh.

S2: —because I couldn't understand how you get that.

The students apparently understood immediately that the problem could be solved by giving a head start to the block that would have the smaller spool. They decided to use spools of size 3 and 4, and correctly determined that with these two spools, the numbers of turns required to move 24 in. would be 8 and 6, respectively. They apparently used the difference of 2 turns to calculate the amount of the head start needed, and had some uncertainty about whether the head start should be 6 or 8 (we conjecture that these numbers were based on the distances that the two blocks would travel in 2 turns). Their conjecture that the head start should be 6 turned out to be correct, as they confirmed by turning the handles and observing that the two blocks were approximately together at 24. Another example, with the same problem, was given by a pair of 11th-graders. After the students gave some solutions involving equal spool sizes, starting locations, and numbers of turns, the interviewer said, "Okay, okay, can you think of any other way? Can you think of a way where you don't have the spools the same size?"

[Example 2, W11.4]

S2: Well, you could put the 3 in and turn that side 3 [red side] 8 times and this one in [point to 6-spool on the blue side] and turn it 4 times.

INT: Okay, great. Is there another way?

S2: You could start them differently. Well, if you—you could do lots of things. You could start red at—

S1: Like you can say you can put a 4-inch on this one [red side] and turn it 6 times and put the 3-inch on that one and turn it 8 times. Or you can put the 4-inch over here [blue side] and the 3-inch over there [red side] and 6 [inaudible].

INT: Okay, what if you had to, let's see—

S2: Or you could do like [inaudible] you could, um, put the 3 in this one [red side] and like a 4 on this one [blue side]. Move this one [red side] 4 times and this one [blue side] 3 times and switch them [the spools] and do the same thing. You can do lots of things. You could do—

INT: Okay, okay, what if you gave the blue block a head start? Then would there be a way that you could do it?

S2: Yeah. Um, well, depending on the head start. I mean you could give it a 6 and then put the 6-spools and run this [blue side] 3 and that [red side] 4. You could move it to 8 and, um, you could, um, yeah. You could, um, put—start the blue one at 8 and put the 4 in [red side] and move this one [handle on blue side] 4 times and that one [handle on red side] 6 times. And they'd there.

INT: You're putting—you're starting the blue one at 8 and you're putting a [blue side]—

S2: 4 in here

INT: 4 and you're going to turn it how many times?

S2: Um—

INT: Say out loud what you're thinking.

S2: —4; well, um, 4 times.

INT: Okay, how did you figure that one out?

S2: Oh, because, um, well, the first time I figured it out was 4 goes into, um, 24 6 times and 4 goes into 8 2 times and so 2 minus 6 is 4 so you have 4 more 4s to go into—you have 4—you need 4 times 8, after 8 to get to 24—

INT: Okay

S2:   —and the second time I just looked and I counted 4, 4, 4, 4 [point to 4-in. increments on ruler on blue side].

These students solved the problem with different numbers of turns to compensate for different spool sizes. When they were asked for a solution with different starting locations they gave a solution with equal spool sizes (6) and different numbers of turns, then gave a different solution with spool sizes of 4 and different numbers of turns.

The second section of the interviews included the following three problems in which a goal was stated and students were asked to find conditions to achieve the goal. For students using the winches, the problems were:

Problem 1:   How can you make the blue block get to 20 ahead of the red block?

Problem 2:   Can you make both blocks get to 24 at the same time?

Problem 3:   Can you make the red block end at 24 and the blue block end at 8?

For students using the tanks, the problems were:

Problem 1:   How could you make the blue tank fill up to 10 before the red tank?

Problem 2:   Can you make both tanks fill up to 12 at the same time?

Problem 3:   Can you make the blue tank fill up to 12 at the same time that the red tank fills up to 4?

After the students gave a solution, the interviewer asked them if they could think of another way to solve the problem. For Problems 1 and 2, the interviewer usually asked for one or more solutions with a constraint; for example, for Problem 1, having equal spool sizes or equal tank sizes.

A summary of the results for the three problems is given in Table 3.1. Distinct solutions were counted if they involved use of different variables; that is, different numerical values for the same variables were not counted as distinct solutions. Solutions could be given in general terms or with numerically specific values; some solutions included both general and specific statements. If the first statement made by a pair of students provided a correct solution, it was scored as "Correct Immediately." If the students expressed uncertainty or confusion and then arrived at a correct answer, it was scored "Correct After Uncertain." If the students gave an incorrect solution but arrived at a correct answer after some discussion, it was scored "Correct After Incorrect." If the discussion of a solution ended without the students giving a correct solution, it was scored "Incorrect." As illustrations, the solution presented as Example 1 included a general statement scored as Correct Immediately and a specific statement that was scored

TABLE 3.1
Numbers of Solutions and Proportions of Statement of Difference Between Values of Variables in Solutions of Problems

Grade and System	Problems Presented	Total Number of Solutions	General or Specific Statements	Number of Solutions	Correct Immed.	Correct After Uncertain	Correct After Incorrect	Incorrect
7, winches	8	19	general	16	.56	.12	.19	.12
			specific	9	.44	.22	.22	.11
7, tanks	10	32	general	22	.77	.18	0	.05
			specific	19	.58	.05	.05	.32
9, winches	23	49	general	24	.96	0	.04	0
			specific	32	.78	.03	.06	.12
9, tanks	11	31	general	22	.86	0	.05	.09
			specific	16	.75	.06	.06	.12
11, winches	11	27	general	13	.92	0	.08	0
			specific	17	.76	.12	.12	0

Correct After Uncertain. Example 2 had two solutions, both with specific statements that were scored as Correct Immediately.

The third section of the interviews asked several questions requiring inferences in situations that were specified. An example involving the tanks was the following, given by a pair of 9th-grade students. The setup has tanks like those in Fig. 3.2, with the blue tanks on the left with the top tank filled to 0 and the bottom tank empty, and the red tanks on the right with the top tank filled to 0 and a starting level of 6 in the bottom tank.

[Example 3, T9.3]

INT: So, if we drain the top two tanks together, will the blue side ever get ahead?

S1 and S2: Yeah.

INT: Okay, when?

S2: That's—you drained 2? That'd be 8—

S1: Okay. They increase—at what point—

INT: [to S2] Why don't you figure it out?

S2: Alright. So say you drain 1 inch there [blue side]. It'd be 4 here [bottom blue], and 8 there [red]. Another 1 inch, that would be at 8 there [blue] and 10 there [red]. Another 1 inch, 12 there [blue], 12 there [red]. Another 1 inch will be 16 [blue] and 14 [red]. Yeah, at—

S1: 14 divided by—

S2: 14 divided by—

S1: 14 minus 6 is—

S2: 14 minus 6 is 8.

S1: Divided by 2—

S2: —by 2 is 4.

S1: 4 inches dropped.

INT: Okay, what level were they equal at?

S2: At what level—

S1: —are they equal?

INT: Yeah, you just figured it out.

S1: About 3 inches dropped from the top.

S2: Yeah.

INT: Oh, and you were telling me after 4 inches, that one's higher [blue]. Okay.

S2: The blue would be higher than the red.

INT: Which side will be higher after 5 turns?

S2: 5 inches?

S1: Ok, didn't we say that at 4 inches, the blue would be greater?

S2: The blue.

S1: Yeah, the blue.

S2: Anywhere after 4 inches, the blue will be greater than the red.

INT: Will the red side ever be higher by 4?

S2: Um—

S1: It is right now. No—

INT: Will the blue side—

S1: By the red side or the blue side?

INT: I'm sorry, will the red side ever be higher by exactly 4?

S2: Will the red side? No.

S1: Wait, yeah. At the first inch, "cause this is gonna go up 2 [red], so that'd bring this one up to—okay. First one's gonna be 4 inches [blue] right?

S2: Mm-hm.

S1: Okay, so this one's [red] gonna have 2 inches, so that's gonna be 8 and 4.

S2: Yeah.

S1: Yeah, it will.

INT: Okay. Will the level on the red side ever be 2 times the level on the blue side?

S2: Um [marks off places on the tank with fingers].

S1: Well, yeah, that's the same thing—same problem.

INT: Okay, yeah, that's fine. Will the level on the red side always be 2 times the level on the blue side?

S2: No.

S1: Proven in problem number—where—

S2: "Cause at 12, they catch—they're the same, and then—

S1: At 4 inches [blue side] is equal to or greater than the level on the red side.

INT: What's that in answer to?

S1: Will the blue ever, no, wait—what was the question?

S2: Will the red ever be twice as much as the blue?

INT: No, I'm asking, "Will the level in the red—" you just told me, in the previous problem, that after 1 inch, red's gonna be twice blue. "Cause that'd be 8 and 4.

S1: But I said that—

INT: Okay, now I'm asking will it always be 2 times?

S1 and S2: No

INT: Okay, now when will it not be?

S2: 2 times?

S1: At 3 inches.

S2: Yeah.

S1: 3 inches dropped from the top.

S2: That'd be 16 there [blue] and that'd be—

S1: [to S2] 3 inches or 2 inches?

S2: Yeah.

The interviews included three questions involving specific inferences. The following was the first question concerning the use of the winches.

Question 1: Let's give the red block a 3-spool and start it at 10; and we'll give the blue block a 4-spool and start it at 5. We'll link the axles together. Now, when you turn the handle, the blue block will catch up to the red block. How many turns will it take for the two to be at the same place?

The following was the first question concerning the use of the tanks

Question 1: On the red side, we have a 6-tank on top and a 3-tank on the bottom, and on the blue side we have a 6-tank on top and a 2-tank on the bottom. The red side starts with 8 on the bottom, and the blue side starts with 4 on the bottom. We'll drain from the top tanks at the same time.
(a) What's going to happen?
(b) Will the level in the blue tank get to be as high as the red tank?—that is, will the blue side catch up with the red side?
(c) How far down will the top tanks be when the bottom tanks have the same height?

The situation for Question 2 with the winches had a 3-spool for the red block and a 6-spool for the blue block. Both blocks started at 0 and the axles were linked.

Question 2: (a) When you turn the handle, will the red block ever get ahead? When will that be? (or Why not?)
(b) How far ahead will the blue block be after 4 turns?
(c) Will the blue block ever be ahead by 6? When will that be? (or Why not?)
(d) Think about the numbers that the two blocks are at as they go along. Will the number that blue is at ever be 2 times the number that red is at? When will that be? (or Why not?)
(e) Will the number that blue is at ever be 3 times the number that red is at? When will that be? (or Why not?)

Question 2 concerning the tanks had 4-tanks on top for both the red and blue sides. The bottom tanks were 1 for the blue side and 2 for the red side. Both bottom tanks were empty.

Question 2: We'll drain the two top tanks together, so their heights are always the same.

    (a) Will the level in the bottom red tank ever be higher than the level in the bottom blue tank? When will that be? (or Why not?)

    (b) How much higher will the blue level be than the red level after you've drained the top tanks down to 5?

    (c) Will the blue level ever be higher than the red level by 4?

    (d) Will the level on the blue side ever be twice as high as the level on the red side? When will that be? (or Why not?)

    (e) Will the level on the blue side ever be 3 times as high as the level on the red side? When will that be? (or Why not?)

Question 3 was parallel to Question 2, except that the two blocks or tanks were unequal at the beginning. In the situation with the winches, the red block had a 3-spool and started at 9; the blue block had a 6-spool and started at 0.

Question 3: (a) Will the blue block ever get ahead? When will that be? (i.e., how many turns will it take?)

           (b) Which block will be ahead after 4 turns? How far ahead will it be?

           (c) Will the red block ever be ahead by 6? When will that be? (or Why not?)

           (d) Will the number that the red block is at ever be 2 times the number that blue is at? When will that be? (or Why not?)

           (e) Will the number that red is at always be 2 times the number that blue is at? When will it be different? (or How do you know?)

With the tanks, the blue side had a 4-tank on top, a 1-tank on the bottom, and the bottom tank was empty. The red side had a 4-tank on top and a 2-tank on the bottom, filled to 6.

Question 3: (a) If we drain the two top tanks together, will the blue side ever get ahead? When will that be? (i.e., How far down will the top tanks be?)

           (b) Which side will be higher after you drain 5 inches? How much higher will it be?

           (c) Will the red side ever be higher by 4? When will that be?

           (d) Will the level on the red side ever be 2 times the level on the blue side? When will that be? (or Why not?)

           (e) Will the level on the red side always be 2 times the level on the blue side? When will it be different? (or How do you know?)

TABLE 3.2
Proportions of Answers to Questions

Question	Grade, System	Questions Presented	Correct Immediately	Correct After Uncertain	Correct After Incorrect	Incorrect
1	7, winches	4	0	.25	.50	.25
	7, tanks	4	.25	0	0	.75
	9, winches	7	.14	0	.14	.71
	9, tanks	4	.25	.50	.25	0
	11, winches	4	.25	.50	.25	0
2	7, winches	19	.74	.16	.11	0
	7, tanks	10	.50	.30	0	.20
	9, winches	33	.64	.18	.06	.12
	9, tanks	14	.57	.36	.07	0
	11, winches	12	.83	0	.17	0
3	7, winches	7	.43	.29	.14	.14
	7, tanks	10	.50	.30	.10	.10
	9, winches	28	.71	.11	.11	.07
	9, tanks	14	.64	.29	.07	0
	11, winches	13	.85	.15	0	0

The answers were scored in the same way as the solutions of problems. The results are summarized in Table 3.2. The numbers in the column "Questions presented" for Question 1 are the numbers of student pairs in each grade who were interviewed with the two systems. In Questions 2 and 3, the number of parts of each question asked to different pairs were summed to obtain the number of "Questions presented," and the data were summed across the five parts of Questions 2 and 3.

I interpret this data as showing that students have significant implicit understanding of quantitative functions that are incorporated in physical systems designed to make relations between quantities easy to grasp. The older students, who had studied algebra for 1 or 2 years, gave more solutions and answers that were correct immediately than the seventh-grade students, but most of the seventh-grade students' answers were correct immediately, and in most other cases they arrived at correct answers after some discussion occurred. As the examples illustrate, conversations by 11th-grade students tended to have crisper numerical reasoning than the younger students.

The similarities between younger and older students were more striking, however, than the differences. All of the students used informal reasoning in solving the problems and answering the questions in almost every case. Attempts to use algebraic notation were extremely rare and never successful. The results are consistent with a hypothesis that students can understand many aspects of functional relations among quantities before they have studied algebra. The point that I hope will be made in this research is that significant mathematical thinking about functions is well within the capabilities of almost all students, even before they have studied the relevant mathematical concepts and principles in formal terms. The causal mechanisms of the systems that we used are easy to understand, and in that case, students can think quite successfully about how the quantities in the systems are related.

EVERYDAY COGNITION

The second research topic that I mention is the study of quantitative reasoning in situations quite different from classrooms. The widespread belief that only a few individuals are "good at math" is sharply contradicted by ethnographic data obtained when individuals are studied in contexts of everyday activity.

Studies of reasoning by youngsters selling produce, candy, or lottery tickets in street markets (Carraher, Carraher, & Schliemann, 1985; Saxe, 1988; 1990), or by young dairy workers assembling collections of products according to order forms (Scribner, 1984), or by shoppers deciding what to buy in supermarkets or dieters deciding on quantities of food (Lave, 1988; Lave, Murtaugh & de la Rocha, 1984) all show that sophisticated reasoning about quantities is a capability that is within the reach of a great many people—perhaps all except a small number of individuals who are disabled in some way. In an example from Saxe (1990), a 12-year-old candy seller in Brazil who had completed the first grade in school was beginning his day with a box filled with 30 candy bars. He paid Cr$8000 for the box, and had set a price of three bars for Cr$1000.

INT: How much will you sell the full box for?
CS: I'll sell the full box for Cr$10,000.
INT: (How do you determine your prices?)
CS: I count like this (illustrating a count of the bars in groups of three by a value of CR$1000). These two (two groups of three) bring Cr$2000, these two (two groups of three) Cr$4000, these two Cr$6000, . . . these two Cr$10,000. I count like this 'cause I'm going to sell the chocolate at three for Cr$1000, and this way the full box will bring Cr$10,000, and my profit will be Cr$2000.
INT: How much will you profit after selling the full box?
CS: Since the box cost me Cr$8000 and I'll sell the full box for Cr$10,000, my profit will be Cr$2000.
INT: Do you think your profit will be good?
CS: It's not going to be very good. But, if I sell two for Cr$1000 it's going to be hard to sell, and if I sold four for Cr$1000, I'd lose too much.
INT: Who taught you to sell chocolate like this?
CS: Nobody. I taught myself. (Saxe, 1990, pp. 223–224)

The research on "everyday math" that is already available supports a conclusion that the apparent lack of mathematical thinking among many school children may have more to do with the way that mathematics is presented in school than it does with the children.

CLASSROOMS AS SETTINGS FOR THINKING

The third topic of research that I consider involves development of novel methods of teaching mathematics in classrooms. In contrast to standard didactic teaching, some teacher-researchers have developed ways to teach in which students are actively involved in thinking collaboratively about the concepts and principles of mathematics, rather than only listening to someone tell them how mathematics should be done.

One current documented example is by Magdalene Lampert (1986, 1990). Lampert teaches a fifth-grade mathematics class, which she has organized in a way that results in students participating in an activity of making sense of mathematical notations and procedures. Here is an excerpt from an example of a class discussion given by Lampert (1990). Lampert was leading a discussion about exponents, examining patterns in the last digit of numbers that are increasing powers of different integers. They had just determined that the last digit in 7^4 is 1, and Lampert asked about the last digit in 7^5.

Arthur: I think it's going to be a 1 again.
Sarah: I think it's 9.
Soo Wo: I think it's going to be 7.
Sam: It *is* a 7.
Teacher (writes on board:
$$7^5 = \quad 1?$$
$$9?$$
$$7?):$$
Arthur, why do you think it's 1?
Arthur: Because 7^4 ends in 1, then it's times 1 again.
Gar: The answer to 7^4 is 2401. You multiply that by 7 to get the answer, so it's 7 times 1.
Teacher: Why 9, Sarah?
Theresa: I think Sarah thought the number should be 49.
Gar: Maybe she thinks it goes 9, 1, 9, 1, 9, 1.
Molly: I know it's 7, 'cause 7 . . .
Abdul: Because 7^4 ends in 1, so if you times it by 7, it'll end in 7.
Martha: I think it's 7. No, I think it's 8.
Sam: I don't think it's 8 because it's odd number times odd number and that's always an odd number.
Carl: It's 7 because it's like saying 49 times 49 times 7.

Arthur: I still think it's 1 because you do 7 times 7 to get 49, and then for 7^4 you do 49 times 49, and for 7^5, I think you'll do 7^4 times itself and that will end in 1.

Teacher: What's 49^2?

Soo Wo: It's 2401.

Teacher: Arthur's theory is that 7^5 should be 2401 times 2401 and since there's a 1 here and a 1 here . . .

Soo Wo: It's 2401 times 7.

Gar: I have a proof that it won't be a 9. It can't be 9, 1, 9, 1, because 7^3 ends in a 3.

Martha: It think it goes, 1, 7, 9, 1, 7, 9, 1, 7, 9.

Teacher: What about 7^3 ending in 3? The last number ends in—9 times 7 is 63.

Martha: Oh . . .

Karl: Abdul's thing isn't wrong, cause it works. He said times the last digit by 7 and the last digit is 9, so the last one will be 3. It's 1, 7, 9, 3, 1, 7, 9, 3.

Arthur: I want to revise my thinking. It would be 7 times 7 times 7 times 7 times 7. I was thinking it would be 7 times 7 times 7 times 7 times 7 times 7 times 7 times 7. (Lampert, 1990, pp. 49–51)

There seems little doubt that these fifth-grade students were engaged in a process of collaborative mathematical thinking. Other teacher-researchers have developed methods of teaching in which students engage in mathematical thinking. Another notable example was Fawcett's (1938) course in geometry, where the students discussed alternative definitions and postulates and each student developed his or her personal version of the system. Schoenfeld (e.g., 1987a) teaches mathematical problem solving to college students, and the students become involved in discussions of alternative methods and the mathematical significance of their results. Lampert's example is especially important in demonstrating that as early as the fifth grade, students can engage in significant mathematical thinking in classroom settings that are appropriately organized.

MATHEMATICAL AND SCIENTIFIC THINKING

An extended discussion of similarities and differences between mathematical and scientific thinking is beyond the scope of this chapter, but a few brief comments are appropriate.

Regarding conceptual competence and everyday cognition, there is a large literature now that emphasizes students' apparent *dis*abilities for learning science, in the form of misconceptions that they are believed to have. It may be, however, that the idea of misconceptions is a misconception that interferes with educators' and cognitive scientists' understanding of students' capabilities for scientific thinking and learning.

An example of the evidence for alleged misconceptions is an answer that many students give when they are asked to draw the path that an object will take if it is dropped from an airplane in flight. Many students draw a straight vertical line, rather than a parabola that takes account of the component of velocity due to the motion of the airplane. This can be interpreted as a belief by the students that the motion of an object is governed by impetus that it receives from an agent, a belief held by Medieval physicists (McCloskey, 1983), and such a belief would be likely to interfere with attempts to teach Newtonian principles of mechanics.

A more optimistic view is provided in a theory that diSessa (1983) is developing. diSessa assumes that people interpret events using schemata that he calls *phenomenological primitives*, or *p-prims*. An example of a p-prim is "force as mover," a tendency to attribute motion to an active force. The "force as mover" p-prim provides an explanation of students' answers that an object will fall down straight from an airplane. diSessa assumes that people have several p-prims, corresponding to different interpretive schemata that are consistent with various aspects of phenomena that they have experienced. Another p-prim is an inertial schema that explains continued motion as a tendency for things to keep moving in the same way they have been moving. In this view, mistakes that are often attributed to misconceptions are more probably due to misapplications or failures to apply appropriate p-prims. For example, the expectation of straight-down motion could be due to applying the "force as mover" p-prim without including the inertial p-prim in one's interpretation, whereas the more nearly correct interpretation would come from applying the "force as mover" and inertial p-prims in combination. Then the correction of students' interpretations could proceed through a process of getting them to interpret the phenomenon in relation to factors that they understand, rather than by requiring a fundamental reconstruction of their beliefs. In general, analyses of students' interpretations of phenomena in terms of p-prims may provide a much more optimistic view of their competence for learning science through activities that involve their actively participating in discourse, based on their own understandings, than the view that is generally found in most of the literature on alleged misconceptions.

Another important issue, raised by Kuhn (1989), concerns an aspect of scientific reasoning that involves understanding the relation between hypotheses and evidence. Kuhn pointed out that scientific thinking includes careful attention to statements that are proposed as hypotheses and evidence that is used to evaluate the hypotheses. Kuhn presented evidence that sixth-grade students treated statements of hypotheses and statements of evidence indiscriminately; in fact, older people, including college students not expert in the domain of the discussion, reasoned less clearly about the relation between hypotheses and evidence than one might hope. A hypothesis suggested by Kuhn's results is that children need to learn a distinction between hypotheses and evidence before it is useful for them to engage in scientific thinking. A similar hypothesis would apply to mathematics, where it is important to distinguish between statements that are made as conjectures or conclusions of arguments and statements that are provided as examples, counterexamples, or proofs of claims. We need research to investigate Kuhn's results more generally. The tasks that she used in her research seem quite artificial, and it may be that there are other tasks, different from hers, in which children would show stronger competence for reasoning discriminatively about general statements and facts or arguments that are used to support or refute them.

Regarding practices of scientific thinking in classrooms, numerous efforts have been made and will continue to be made to develop classroom settings in which students participate actively in empirical studies and theoretical discussions. These include hands-on science materials that are used for activities in which students construct demonstrations of physical principles and discussion-based science teaching in which students offer hypotheses and discuss their implications and evidence that supports or disconfirms them (Hatano & Inagaki, in press).

CONCLUSIONS

This chapter advocates a policy of adopting a thinking curriculum for the teaching of mathematics and science in school to all children. This policy issue includes many questions, and I have addressed one of them: the question of whether children are capable of participating productively in activities of mathematical and scientific thinking so that they could learn to think in these disciplines by doing it. The major claim of the chapter is that they are.

The evidence supporting this claim is encouraging, but very preliminary. I presented a sample of evidence for the claim in the domain of high-school algebra, consisting of examples and summaries of scores of performance in interviews that show that students have significant informal understanding of functional relations among quantities in some physical systems. This is consistent with other evidence about children's conceptual competence in domains of number, physical causality, and some biological and cognitive concepts. The evidence, however, is fragmentary. We need more detailed and systematic investigations of the topics that have been studied, and investigations of topics that have not yet been examined. The evidence we have now is also largely descriptive, and we need to develop more powerful theoretical analyses that support argumentation about the implications of general principles that can be used as guides to educational development and practice.

I also mentioned evidence regarding two other parts of the question of competence, in addition to competence for understanding concepts. I mentioned an example of research on everyday cognition, which shows that significant competence for reasoning about quantities is widespread among people, rather than being limited to those relatively few whose performance in school mathematics tasks shows outstanding success in understanding and reasoning. And I mentioned an example of research on classroom practice, which shows that children are capable of participating productively in a discourse that is organized to produce shared understanding of notations, phenomena, concepts, and principles. Both the study of everyday cognition and of classroom practices are in very early stages of development, compared with the bodies of research and theory that are in place for the understanding of students' performance on problems used traditionally in school mathematics and science (see, e.g., Gardner et al., 1990; Smith, 1991), and of the variables that influence effectiveness of teachers in traditional didactic settings (Brophy & Goode, 1986).

In addition to questions about student capabilities, the issue of adopting a thinking curriculum for mathematics and science involves questions of student motivation and many questions of institutional practices, including teachers' capabilities and the nature of teachers' work, methods of assessing students' learning, the social and institutional organization of schooling, the goals that the society has for its educational system, and methods of evaluating schools, setting levels of financial support, and accountability. The cognitive questions addressed in this chapter are part of the issue, but they need to be integrated with a host of other questions if we are to build a coherent base of scientific support for a fundamental change in educational practice.

It would be inappropriate, of course, to wait until all the evidence is in before anyone works for fundamental reform of our practices of mathematics and science education. The best course, in all probability, is to invest significant energy in reforming classroom practice, teacher education, curriculum materials, assessment practices, and school organization, along with a significant investment in the scientific study of the cognitive, affective, social, and institutional processes that we need to understand.

The findings that we have in hand provide encouraging support for educational reform that would include more thinking activity by students in their scientific and mathematical learning. Based on these results, preliminary as they are, mathematical and scientific thinking are activities that students are quite capable of; indeed, they engage in them naturally and successfully even in advance of learning the formal versions of the concepts that they use. This suggests an approach to learning in mathematics and science that would turn the usual curriculum on its head. It would treat thinking as a basic ingredient of learning, and would involve constructing situations that support mathematical or scientific thinking by students, in groups and as individuals, that would provide them with opportunities to construct mathematical and scientific ideas meaningfully as a major part of their school activity. This would be a very different kind of mathematics and science education than we currently provide for most students, and it seems worth working on.

ACKNOWLEDGMENTS

Prepared for a symposium on higher-order thinking in mathematics and science subject-matter learning at AAAS, January, 1989. This research was supported by the National Science Foundation, grant BNS-8718918. Other participants in the project include Joyce Moore, Meg Korpi, Jean-Luc Gurtner, and Greg Pribyl. I have presented some of these ideas elsewhere, in a presentation to the North American Chapter of the International Group for the Psychology of Mathematics Education (Greeno, 1988) and in a symposium at the Cognitive Science Society (Greeno, 1991).

4

Expert Knowledge and Processes of Thinking

Robert Glaser
Learning Research and Development Center
University of Pittsburgh

Highly competent performance is intrinsically fascinating, regardless of whether we witness it in memory experts, quiz kids, Olympic players, medical diagnosticians, chess masters, or mathematicians and biophysicists. In the past 15 years or so, describing competence and the processes that underlie it has become a significant endeavor in the study of human cognition. The tactic in these studies has been to explore the well-established performances that proficient people display, which have developed over time, and the components and properties of knowledge and skill that characterize highly competent performance. The results of this work define objectives for human attainment—goals for learning that can inform teaching practices at all levels. Expertise is proficiency taken to its highest level, and understanding of the experts' hard-won knowledge and skill can be used to foster the novices' progress and, perhaps, to expand the proficiencies of experts themselves.

The seeds for work on expertise were sown in the widely cited Newell and Simon (1972) book, *Human Problem Solving*. Newell and Simon described the observations of Adrian de Groot, a famous Dutch chess master who compared chess masters' and novice chess players' accounts of their thinking as they confronted various chess problems (de Groot, 1965, 1966). de Groot's findings anticipated key ideas in our current understanding of the nature of expertise. Although de Groot was unsuccessful in attempting to distinguish stronger from weaker players' performances using various assessments of memory or facility with the general problem-solving heuristics, he succeeded in identifying a critical difference by asking them, after 5 second's viewing, to recall and reproduce the positions of chess pieces that would occur in a game. Experts reproduced the board layouts perfectly, but this ability was less apparent in weaker players. Pure

63

memory capacity was not involved, for strong and weak players alike had trouble remembering randomly arranged layouts of chess pieces; rather, perceptual abilities and knowledge organization clearly were characteristic of highly competent players. Strong players automatically viewed particular configurations of pieces as laden with meaning: A given configuration suggested possible moves and helped the player anticipate the consequences of those moves.

The perceptual aspects of problem solving in chess seem to be crucial. Research that has followed up on de Groot's work has shown that chess masters recognize clusters of related pieces as familiar constellations and they store each cluster in memory as a single symbol or pattern. Less-skilled players have to describe the board as a larger number of simpler patterns—hence, they cannot hold in memory all of the information required to reproduce a layout. When the same number of pieces is arranged in a scrambled pattern on the board, few of the resulting configurations are familiar even to grandmasters. They then need more symbols to describe the position than they can hold simultaneously in short-term memory—hence, their recall is as poor as weaker players'. Chess masters, thus, do not show greater memory capacity for chess pieces in general, but only for the board's instantiations of chess principles as they crop up in a game. The quantities of patterns demanded by their expertise are of a high order of magnitude. In the many years required to attain chess mastery, a player might be expected to acquire a "vocabulary" of subpatterns comparable in extent to the verbal knowledge required to read English (Chase & Simon, 1973).

The study of expert/novice differences in other domains has deepened our appreciation of the significance of the experts' perceptions of patterns. This perceptiveness, we can now suggest, is one of the critical manifestations of experts' highly organized, integrated structures of knowledge. In electronics, for example, skilled technicians reconstructing symbolic drawings of circuit diagrams do so according to the functional nature of the elements in the circuit, such as amplifiers, rectifiers, and filters. Novice technicians, however, reconstruct the diagrams on the basis of the spatial proximity of the elements (Egan & Schwartz, 1979).

Expert radiologists' readings of x-rays show that the expert first builds a mental representation of possible abnormalities and that this representation guides the diagnosis and must satisfy tests of applicability before it is allowed to control viewing and interpretation. The expert works efficiently to reach a stage where an appropriate general model or schema guides the diagnosis. Less-expert interns do not confirm the applicability of the patterns they invoke, and an incomplete model may be triggered and control their efforts (Lesgold et al., 1988).

Like the chess results, such evidence shows that the expert in a domain takes in and uses information in *chunks*—in organizations and integrations of knowledge, or meaningful patterns—extremely rapidly. Whether the domain is chess configurations, functional interpretations of circuit diagrams, or representations of anatomical abnormalities in x-rays, the central underlying properties or meaningful deep structure of the situation is key to experts' perceptions, whereas the surface features and structural properties (such as proximity and literal descriptive aspects) organize the less-than-expert individuals' perceptions.

This aspect of expertise has been investigated in studies of scientific problem solving. In experiments where novices and experts were asked to classify a set of elementary physics mechanics problems in terms of the requirements for solutions, the two groups tackled the task on entirely different bases. The novices used surface features to group rotation problems, inclined plane problems, or spring problems in their classifications. In contrast, the experts grouped problems that had little surface resemblance; they saw as similar problems that involved the principle of conservation of energy or Newton's second law. The experts were able to tie the surface features of problems to deeper principles, and inducing these principles was predictive of fast, efficient, and accurate methods of solution (Chi, Glaser, & Rees, 1982).

Another observable difference between expert and novice problem solvers' performances is their pause-times for retrieving successive equations. Experts appear to invoke sets of equations; eliciting one equation activates rapid retrieval of related equations. Novices do not exhibit such chunking in setting up equations. It appears that, for experts, physics equations are stored in functional configurations, so that accessing one procedure leads to another (Larkin, 1979).

The results of research to date has made it clear that experts' knowledge structures play a critical role in their performances. Experts, as the studies mentioned indicate, have a great deal of domain-specific information, and this information is highly organized and conceptually integrated. This organized knowledge appears to account for the experts' capacities for rapid pattern recognition and categorization.

Coordinate with these abilities, experts in science and math often make use of qualitative reasoning to approach a problem that will require quantitative solution. Expert physicists, for example, appear to exercise a form of *physical intuition* (Simon & Simon, 1978) prior to their retrieval of equations—that is, before they even consider calculations or specific solution procedures. In contrast, novices rush into quantitative manipulations and plug in formulas (Larkin, McDermott, Simon, & Simon, 1980b; McDermott & Larkin, 1978). This initial qualitative phase of problem solving is key in the investigation of expert performance.

One aspect of such qualitative analysis is the representation of a problem in terms of a *runnable mental model*. This model specifies the main causal connections of the components of a situation and, like other aspects of problem representation, has a formative influence on performance. For example, in a statics problem involving a ladder leaning against a wall, the mental model would probably include the ladder, the floor, the wall, and the points of contact, as well as gravity and the forces operating at points of contact. Once this kind of representation has been constructed in memory and the expert has a feel for the situation, the equations of equilibrium can be constructed readily (Simon & Simon, 1978).

Research on algebra students' initial representations of problems is revealing here. In confronting pseudo word-problems (i.e., problems about physically unrealizable situations), a few highly proficient students immediately perceived the incongruity in the problems (Paige & Simon, 1966). The rest proceeded to invoke equations before realizing that the solutions would be meaningless (e.g., a negative quantity would be obtained for the length of an object). The good solvers apparently constructed a representation that provided a basis for inferences about problem features and their relations that were not available from the problem statement. This model gave them a basis for questioning the problem content and monitoring applicability of solution procedures.

SIX GENERALIZATIONS

In general, then, experts' highly integrated structures of knowledge lie behind many salient features of their performances. Current understanding of expertise now allows a set of generalizations about its nature. The implications and impact of experts' knowledge are far reaching in shaping their thinking, as these generalizations indicate.

1. *Experts' proficiency is very specific.* The precision of experts' performances derives from the specialized knowledge that drives their reasoning. Specificity of performance is evidenced by the disruption of proficiency in instances where random or meaningless patterns or poorly structured problems are presented. Under these conditions, experts lose their rapid perceptual and representational ability and resort to general problem-solving strategies. It may be, however, that certain task domains are more generalizable than others, so that adults who are experts in applied mathematics or aesthetic design, or younger students who have learned measurement and quantitative concepts, have transferable forms of expertise. Nevertheless, competence in one domain is no guarantee of effectiveness in others.

2. *Experts perceive large, meaningful patterns.* These patterns guide experts' thinking in everyday working activities. Pattern recognition occurs so rapidly that it appears to take on the character of intuition. In contrast, the patterns that novices recognize are smaller, less articulated, more literal and surface-oriented, and far less related to abstracted principles. Like other aspects of experts' performance, this extraordinary representational ability depends on the organization of knowledge existing in memory.

3. *Experts' problem solving entails selective search of memory or use of general problem-solving tactics.* Whereas novices display a good deal of

search and processing of a general nature, experts' fast-access pattern recognition and representational capability facilitate approaches to problems that reduce the roles of these processes. Even where it can be assumed that experts and novices have similar cognitive capacities, the experts' performances have an efficiency that derives primarily from their knowledge being structured for retrieval, pattern recognition, and inferencing.

4. *Experts' knowledge is highly procedural and goal-oriented.* In experts' highly structured knowledge base, concepts are bound to procedures and the rules and conditions for their application. This functional knowledge is closely tied to knowledge of the goal structure of a problem. Experts and novices may be equally competent at recalling small specific (multiple-choice type) items of domain-related information, but high-knowledge individuals far more readily relate these items of information in cause-and-effect sequences that link the goals and subgoals needed for problem solution.

5. *Experts' knowledge enables them to use self-regulatory processes with great skill.* Experts proficiently monitor their own problem-solving activities; they have the ability to step back, so to speak, at appropriate points, and observe their solution processes and the outcomes of their performances. Their self-awareness is also shown in their allocation of attention and their sensitivity to information feedback as they work. Use of self-regulatory processes sometimes slows experts as they initially encode a difficult problem, although they are faster problem solvers overall. Here, novices' reliance on surface features allows them speed initially.

6. *Experts' proficiency can be routinized or adaptive.* Competence is influenced by the task demands and by the conditions for work; thus, experts' attained proficiencies can be context-bound. Under some conditions, maybe most, their performances become routinized as well as efficient and accurate. Under others, experts develop the capability for *opportunistic planning,* which is manifested by their revising problem representations readily and accessing multiple possible interpretations of a situation. The conditions and demands of education and of work can foster combinations of highly competent routine and adaptive expertise.

A NOTE ON EXPERT PERFORMANCES IN UNFAMILIAR TERRITORY

The picture of expertise presented thus far does not take into account the competence (or perhaps the lack of competence) that experts demonstrate when they work at the frontiers of knowledge—when the problems they confront are from unfamiliar domains or are not well structured, so that patterns and solution procedures cannot readily be perceived.

Working such problems—which can be called *ill-structured problems* or *problems of discovery*—requires: (a) the resolution of open constraints; (b) decisions about imposing parameter values that are entailed in the problem presentation or conceptualization; (c) a search for analogies; and (d) most importantly, pursuit of equivalents to the powerful principles that underlie solutions for well-structured or familiar problems. In these novel situations, the definition of subproblems for which patterns can be seen that enable particular approaches is a key step. The solver must invent an organization that synthesizes potential understandings—that is, the solver must come up with some representation or model as a basis for proceeding (Simon, 1973; Voss & Post, 1988).

What is of interest here is that, somewhat like novices, experts bring *general* problem-solving processes to bear. They do decompose an ill-structured problem into a better structured set of subproblems, but with greater facility than a novice would. They also are able to select parameter values for open constraints that lead to a possible meaningful solution by supplying testable candidate problem representations. In general, where problems do not yield to straightforward approaches, experts can usefully resort to analogies with systems they understand well and search for matches and mismatches. They may attempt to impose some model of the workings of another phenomenon on the problem at hand to try to understand how the model would behave in the new context. They may pose extreme-case arguments or construct simpler problems of a similar sort and bring those solutions to the original problem.

This use of general heuristics does not take on significance as a substitute for domain knowledge. On the contrary, general heuristics serve mostly in the attempt to gain access to domain knowledge that can be used for problem solution. In a sense, the use of general heuristics reflects the attempt to move ill-structured problems of discovery into the familiar domain where extant knowledge can be brought into play. Rather than using general heuristics in a decontextualized way—as free-floating interrogators of a situation—the expert uses them to make contact with available knowledge and the solution processes it might afford. The abstract use of general heuristics in courses on thinking skills or reasoning may not be successful for this reason.

EXPERTISE AND WRITING SKILL

As an illustration of how the properties of expertise interact, the domain of writing competence is interesting. An increasing amount of analysis is being undertaken on the nature of novice and expert writing. Writing is a skill that we must rely on in much of our schooling and working lives. It is a basic skill of educated people, yet involves, it seems, a neverending process of acquiring competence. Writing can be viewed as a form of domain-specific problem solving; through structuring and expressing our ideas in written texts, we think and learn to think in our fields. For these reasons, it is an apt arena in which to examine the interdependence of the various aspects of expert performance. Consider then the specificity, integrated knowledge, problem representation, task monitoring, and goal orientation of experts' performances in writing.

Specificity

Writing, in a fundamental way, requires linguistic knowledge, that is, a strong vocabulary; a good grasp of grammar and syntax; and an awareness of rhythm, voice, and figures of speech. The student, the poet, the playwright, and the novelist all develop this knowledge, more or less, as does the academician or scientist writing about research. The domain specificity of writing expertise is now widely acknowledged by teachers and educators. In an illuminating analysis of the import of this for education, David Bartholomae observed that:

> Every time a student sits down to write for us, he has to invent the university for the occasion—invent the university or a branch of it, that is, like history or anthropology, or economics, or biology. He has to learn to speak our language, to speak as we do, to try on the peculiar ways of knowing, selecting, evaluating, reporting, concluding, and arguing that define the discourse of our community. . . . [a student must learn] to work within fields where the rules governing the presentation of an example or the development of an argument are both distinct and (often), even to a professional, mysterious. (Bartholomae, 1985, p. 4)

Bartholomae pointed out that, while in introductory writing courses, students are concerned with university discourse in its most generalized form. Expertise in writing, in the longer term, requires students to locate themselves in disciplinary forms of discourse that are not immediately accessible. Those who can write reasonably coherent expositions in one domain, say, political science, may be incoherent when faced with crafting an essay in sociology or philosophy. This is not unlike the loss manifested by experts when they are required to operate outside of their disciplines.

Integrated Knowledge

Writing expertise requires substantial declarative and procedural knowledge. Students who are novice writers in a domain are not necessarily inept thinkers; they are rather insufficiently familiar not only with information about specialized topics but also with the specific conventions or techniques of expository discourse—the procedures for describing and arguing for an interpretation or for presenting claims and counterclaims. The patterns of reasoning that we expect in academic writing are not inherent in our thinking; they are conventional, learnable forms of argumentation and rhetoric.

For example, student writers must learn to support the generalizations on which their reasoning hinges. As novices, they may not be aware that they must explicate how examples and illustrations support generalizations. Proficient writing requires sophisticated forms of this sensitivity to grounding generalizations, interpretations, and claims. Writing knowledge also includes responsiveness to the intended audience; proficient writers shape their prose differently for specialists or for informed generalists. These forms of writing knowledge are rather specific to the task and comprise the integrated knowledge that underlies proficiency.

Representation

In writing, the initial representation of the task is highly influential (Flower, Hayes, Carey, Schriver, & Stratman, 1986). The individual's perceptions of the aims of a piece of writing largely determine the nature of subsequent revision, and revision, of course, is where the real work goes on. Perspectives on the task can be of a local and shallow nature or of a global and more meaningful nature. Consequently, inexperienced and experienced writers make different kinds of changes in the course of revision. Novices typically focus on the conventions and rules of writing, but more advanced students make many changes, including a significant number that affect the text's meaning. Here, again, surface as opposed to deeper problem representations characterize novices' performances: Novice writers work on surface features, using word and punctuation deletion and addition as important strategies; experienced writers conceptualize the task as a wholistic enterprise that may require elaborating the treatment of a point, insuring the effectiveness of argument structure, and estimating the utility of shifts in voice as well as checking grammar and punctuation.

As noted, expert/novice studies in various domains have shown that experts arrive at solutions quickly in problem-solving tasks, although they often appear to spend more time in the initial process of problem representation than novices. Studies of revision suggest that novice writers do not approach this task as a time-consuming, recursive one. They make little use of their drafts, making most of their changes as they produce the text; they hardly reread their papers before they begin a new version. Experts spend a significant portion of their time rereading their drafts in the attempt to develop more complete representation of the problems that must be attacked, and thus this aspect of revision is one to which instruction should attend (Bridwell, 1980; Flower et al., 1986).

Representation of the problems to be attacked in revision can be accomplished in two ways. First, there is a monitoring and evaluation process that builds up a representation that carries with it information and strategies for solving the problem. Second, there is a more immediate categorization or pattern recognition process that occurs quickly. In the first kind of representation (Flower et al., 1986), experienced writers monitor their progress; they observe the features of their draft, search the possible writing strategies in their repertoires, and focus on an appropriate goal, for example, decide whether to work at the level of the whole text or at a more syntactic proofreading level. A representation of the task is generated from this interplay between the analysis of text features and the student's store of knowledge about revision strategies and currently attainable goals.

The second kind of representation requires rapid categorization of a particular task to be accomplished. Like experts in other areas, the good writer must learn to recognize a wide array of patterns. Recognition of a familiar pattern brings forth the strategies and goals applicable to it, just as board patterns do for chess masters and x-ray patterns do for expert radiologists. Proficient writers, because of their stores of knowledge, employ problem classifications that go beyond superficial features to the deeper structure of text meaning and presentation. As noted, this rapid categorization of situations takes on the character of intuitive performance.

Task Monitoring and Goal Orientation

In carrying out revision, experts show a significant sensitivity to task demands and to features of prose; they match their performances to the goals entailed in their representation of the task. Sometimes, a subgoal at a particular level is chosen because a more complex or complete goal is not attainable at the moment. This may be done to simplify the task at hand, to get on with it, so that more complex goals can be eventually attained. At other times, the demands of a task are such that proficient writers see no reason for working at a complex level when a goal requiring less level of effort will suffice, and their technique is adjusted accordingly. Inexperienced writers are less facile in generating goals suitable to a portion of a task or in adjusting to the task required. Their subgoal analysis is superficial, with the result that changes appropriate to the text are never addressed. Thus, analysis of subgoals of revision should be a significant focus of instruction.

Writing competence, like other forms of expertise, probably ranges along a continuum from routine or conventional expertise to adaptive expertise. Routine experts are outstanding in terms of speed, accuracy, and automaticity of performance; they construct mental models convenient and efficient for performing their tasks, but they may lack adaptability when faced with new kinds of problems. Repeated application of a procedure, with little variation, can lead to routine expertise. Adaptive expertise requires variation and is encouraged by playful situations and educational settings and experiences where understanding and transfer are valued along with efficient performance (Hatano & Inagaki, 1986).

IMPLICATIONS FOR TEACHING AND RESEARCH

What do the accruing findings on expertise generally suggest for teaching and designing experiences for students that will enable them to attain high levels of competence in the various domains of knowledge? Four points seem essential: the nature of practice, the development of self-monitoring and of principled performance, and the social context of learning.

The Nature of Practice

Obviously, proficiency is a matter of experience and practice requiring highly motivated learners who spend long hours and do the hard work necessary. But there is more to practice than motivation. Practice, as it comes about in the usual course of training, is not necessarily very efficient. On the basis of our knowledge of the specific aspects of competence and expertise, we are now able to find ways to compress or shortcut experience, or at least to present experience in more systematic fashion so that its impact is optimized. These findings suggest that practice should focus on situations where there are complex patterns to be perceived, and where recognition of these patterns implies particular moves and procedures for solution. An organized sequence of increasingly complex forms of pattern recognition tasks, associated with their procedural meaning, might be developed in sequences of instruction. For example, such experiences have been designed for technical training, including components of the job of air traffic control (Schneider, 1985), for geometry (Anderson, Boyle, & Yost, 1985), and for electronic trouble shooting (Lesgold et al., 1988).

A consideration in designing practice is its resulting in automaticity for some components of competence, that is, in the ability to perform certain actions with little conscious thought. If practice produces this automaticity, then an individual has greater memory processing capability available to engage in parts of the task that require conscious thought, such as re-representing a problem or self-monitoring performance. Automatic processes are very apparent in competent performers; skilled readers can decode words with little conscious thought and, as a result, have greater cognitive space left over for interpreting the meaning of a text. The point here is that practice must continue until certain aspects of behavior become effortless when carried on as part of a larger exercise. Situations that assess students' progress toward some proficient performance, therefore, must not test component skills separately because, although performed adequately when tested by themselves, taken in combination, some components might interfere with other aspects of the larger task (Glaser, 1981).

The value of practice can be increased, if we see it as something to be carefully designed. Much learning in elementary physics is thought to take place as students practice by solving the problems at the end of textbook chapters. These are usually done as homework assignments that may later be illustrated on the blackboard in the classroom. But, the opportunity for sustained, guided practice—practice in which the student sees the principles that relate groups of problems and links them to the procedures required for those problems—is rarely afforded. To optimize teaching, we need to design practice in which learners are encouraged to search for the important connections between principles and procedures (Chi, Bassok, Lewis, Reimann, & Glaser, 1989).

Self-Monitoring

Because self-monitoring—the ability to observe and, if necessary, reshape one's performance—is a hallmark of expertise, this skill should be emphasized in instruction. The work of Alan Schoenfeld (1985) has opened up new ideas for teaching self-monitoring heuristics in the context of learning mathematical problem solving. Heuristics are taught in a contextualized way that makes contact with the students' mathematics knowledge base. One aspect of Schoenfeld's work involves the teaching and demonstration of control or management strategies that make explicit such processes as generating alternative courses of action, evaluating which course can be carried out and whether it can be managed in the time available, and assessing progress. The students learn to monitor and direct their activity by asking such questions as: What am I doing now? Am I making progress? What else could I be doing instead? Through demonstrations and practice, students focus on critical decisions and actions at strategic levels as well as on the rote specifics of the solution.

Furthermore, Schoenfeld has directly confronted the issue of imparting an appropriate belief system about the interpretive nature of mathematical problem solving. During the process of learning mathematics, students begin to realize that searches often come to dead ends; exploration of possible heuristics and different paths does not guarantee solution. He challenges his students to find difficult problems for him to solve, so they can observe his own struggles and floundering, which legitimate students' floundering as well. Students begin to realize that mathematics requires neither merely recognizing principles, nor merely applying procedures, but, rather, a creative interpretive process of exploration and reasoning. The student's adopting this view seems especially helpful when problem representations are not readily constructed, and revisions of equations and procedures are needed so that adequate solutions can be carried out.

Principled Performance

Education also must emphasize that the most salient and ubiquitous hallmark of expertise—whether in chess, writing, science, or mathematics—is principled performance. Performance takes place not only with well-learned procedural knowledge, but also in a space for thought—in the context of a model, a theory, or a principle that guides performance through constraints and structures for inference, and allows competent individuals to avoid disconnected trial and error (Greeno & Simon, 1988). This permits understanding of one's performance, the swift and graceful recovery from error, and the seizing of opportunities for more elegant and precise solution and discovery. Expertise then becomes more than a matter of sheer efficiency and, as it is acquired, knowledge becomes an object for questioning and learning from experience and, thereby, is reorganized to enable new thought and action. An essential aim of instruction and the design of curriculum materials should be to enable the student to acquire structured knowledge along with procedural skill. Too often the fragmented bits of information supplied by textbook and teaching presentations do not encourage students to construct organized knowledge usable for thinking and principled performance.

The Social Context of Learning

A fourth aspect of cognition that should be emphasized as central to change in educational practice turns us away from internal cognition alone to the influence of the situation in which learning occurs. Cognitive activity in school and outside is inseparable from a cultural milieu. The acquisition of competent performance takes place in an interpersonal system in which participation and guidance from others influences the understanding of new situations and the management of problem solving that leads to learning. Certain theories of human development have emphasized the social genesis of learning (Vygotsky, 1978). Conceptual development involves internalizing cognitive activities experienced in social settings, and many studies have pointed out the motivational variables involved in shared responsibility for thinking that enhance learning in group settings (Brown & Campione, in press; Brown & Palincsar, 1989).

From a cognitive perspective, a group can serve several roles. First, it extends the locus of self-monitoring activity by providing triggers for cognitive dissatisfaction outside the individual. An audience monitors individual thinking, opinions, and beliefs, and can elicit explanations that clarify points of difficulty. Moreover, the learner's exposure to alternative points of view challenges his or her initial understanding. In addition, with the help of advanced peers or a teacher who provide supportive scaffolding, the collaborative group maintains a mature version of a target task. By sharing it, a complex task is made more manageable, yet is not over-simplified. Each learner contributes what he or she can and gains from the contributions of those more expert. In this context, to use Vygotsky's term, a zone of proximal development is created where learners perform within their range of competence while being assisted in realizing their potential levels of higher performance.

A most salient aspect in a social context for learning is the elevation of thinking to an overt, observable status. As students participate in group roles, various problem-solving procedures, strategies of reasoning, and techniques for accomplishing goals become apparent. This reality is to be compared with classroom learning where thinking may be rarely an observable enterprise and opportunities for its shaping through external influences are limited. Thus, school instruction might well consider how teaching practice can make apparent the forms of student's thinking, in ways that can be observed, transmitted, discussed, reflected on, and moved toward more competent performance and dispositions for reasoning.

In conclusion, it should be emphasized that, for the most part, investigations of the nature of expertise have emphasized the characteristics of the performance system and not the learning and developmental processes through which performance is attained. Research must now turn to the study of conditions for learning. Undoubtedly, the significant contributions of the methods and the results produced by the analysis of complex human competence will contribute to this work. Investigation of learning processes in a pursuit of well-specified principles for instruction are accelerating (Glaser & Bassok, 1989). Significant studies are under way of instructional programs that facilitate the transition from declarative to more proceduralized functional knowledge (Anderson, Farrell, & Sauers, 1984; Lewis, Milson, & Anderson, 1988), the use of self-regulatory processes that foster learning and understanding (Brown & Palincsar, 1989; Collins, Brown, & Newman, 1989), and the processes of knowledge interrogation that contribute to the development of the structured knowledge that enables expert problem solving (Clancey, 1986; White & Frederiksen, 1986). With the expansion of experimental programs that are grounded in well-articulated instructional principles, both theoretical and applied work on learning will gain in precision and effectiveness. With studies of expertise as the groundwork, a science of learning can make the path to proficiency one that is well marked and can be more readily followed than ever before.

ACKNOWLEDGEMENT

Preparation of this article was sponsored in part by the national Center for Student Learning at the Learning Research and Development Center of the University of Pittsburgh. The national Center for Student Learning is funded by the Office of Educational Research and Improvement of the U.S. Department of Education.

5 Enhancing Higher-Order Thinking Skills in Physics

Jose P. Mestre
Robert J. Dufresne
William J. Gerace
Pamela T. Hardiman
Jerold S. Tougher*
University of Massachusetts, Amherst

In this chapter we discuss the acquisition of expertise in physics. More specifically, we present a series of studies that investigated the potential of performing structured problem analyses for modifying the problem-solving behavior of novice physics students to more nearly resemble behavior observed in expert physicists. As pointed out in Glaser's excellent review chapter (chap. 4 in this volume), considerable effort has been devoted to mapping out the cognitive processes employed by experts and novices engaged in complex problem-solving tasks. The belief underlying this type of research is that the information gleaned from studying the problem-solving behavior at the endpoints of the expertise dimension can be used to devise instructional approaches aimed at making the transition from novice to expert more efficient. To date, relatively few studies have evaluated approaches for promoting behavior observed in experts.

Previous studies focusing on evaluating treatments aimed at promoting expert-like behavior are of two types. In one type of study, one or a few topics from a scientific domain become the focus of the investigation and a treatment is designed to promote some specific aspect of expertise. The effectiveness of the treatment is measured in terms of improvements on a cognitive task designed to measure some well-known trait of expertise (e.g., problem-solving performance or degree of reliance on principles in problem-solving tasks). The task is administered before and after the treatment, and the degree of improvement is used to gauge the effectiveness of the focal treatment relative to some control treatment(s). For example, one study in physics found that novices improved their recall and problem-solving performance following a focal treatment in which a

---

*Permanent affiliation, Science Division, Curry College.

few physics topics were presented in a hierarchical manner, similar to the way experts are known to store their knowledge in memory (Eylon & Reif, 1984). Another study in which novices were taught to conduct qualitative analyses (similar to those conducted by experts) of Newton's Second Law problems resulted in improved problem-solving performance on similar problems (Heller & Reif, 1984).

The focus of the other type of study is to promote improvements in performance over a wide range of topics in a domain. Because of the breadth and scope of the topics covered, the treatments used in this type of study are generally much longer in duration. One such study in mathematics, conducted by Schoenfeld and Herrmann (1982), evaluated the effectiveness of a semester-long problem-solving course in which college students were explicitly taught problem-solving strategies used by experts. This protracted treatment produced marked improvements in problem-solving performance and in reliance on principles in categorizing problems according to their similarity of solution.

The purpose of our studies is to investigate the changes in problem-solving behavior that result from a focal treatment in which novices practice performing problem analyses similar to those performed by experts. This treatment consists of constraining novices to perform hierarchical, qualitative analyses of problems based on principles and procedures that could be applied to solve them. Our studies differ from the two types just described in that the treatment is relatively brief, yet it covers a wide range of physics topics. To evaluate this treatment, several cognitive tasks designed to measure different aspects of expertise were administered before and after treatment.

We begin with a description of the focal treatment and another treatment used for control purposes. We then discuss studies evaluating the effectiveness of the focal treatment in terms of its ability to produce manifestations of expert-like behavior in three areas: (a) judgments of solution similarity, (b) use of principle-based reasoning, and (c) problem-solving performance. We conclude with a discussion of the instructional implications of the findings.

DESCRIPTION OF COMPUTER-BASED TREATMENTS

Two of the treatments used in our studies were implemented in computer-based environments described later in this chapter. One computer-based environment incorporated an expert-like approach to solving problems; we call this environment the Hierarchical Analysis Tool (HAT), and it was used as the focal treatment. The other computer-based treatment was based on a novice-like formulaic approach; we call this environment the Equation Sorting Tool (EST).

Description of the Hierarchical Analysis Tool (HAT)

The approach incorporated in the HAT is consistent with the types of analyses that experts perform while they are engaged in solving problems (Chi, Feltovich,

& Glaser, 1981; Larkin, 1981; Larkin, McDermott, Simon, & Simon, 1980a). The HAT is a menu-driven environment, implemented on IBM-PCs, that employs a hierarchical framework for performing qualitative analyses of problems based on principles and procedures. The word "tool" in the name is meant to imply that the environment facilitates constructing a problem's solution, rather than actually supplying the answer. The HAT does not present or teach content— it simply allows the user to practice a principle-based problem-solving approach.

To analyze a problem, the user answers well-defined questions by making selections from menus that are dynamically generated by software. In the first menu, the user is asked to select one of four general principles that could be applied to solve the problem under consideration. Subsequent menus focus on ancillary concepts and procedures, and are dependent on the prior selections made. When the analysis is complete, the HAT provides a set of equations that is consistent with the menu selections made during the analysis. If the analysis is carried out appropriately, then these equations could be used to generate a solution to the problem; however, the user must still manipulate the equations to answer the exact question asked in the problem. If the analysis is carried out incorrectly (i.e., the user makes inappropriate selections for the problem under consideration), then the final equations are consistent with the choices made, but inappropriate for solving the problem.

It is important to note that the HAT neither tutors nor provides feedback to the user—it merely constrains the type and order of questions that should be considered when analyzing a problem. Further, the HAT's functioning is independent of the problem being analyzed. That is, the HAT has no knowledge of the problem being worked on by the user, nor does it present problems for the user to analyze. In short, the HAT can be thought of as an elaborate, hierarchical tree-like structure; the exact path that a user takes to analyze a problem depends on the selections made at each juncture along the way.

An example will help to illustrate how the HAT could be used to analyze a typical problem. Figure 5.1 provides an example of the series of menus and choices that would correctly analyze the problem in Fig. 5.2 (each menu is presented one at a time on the computer screen). The "prompt line" at the bottom of each screen allows the user various options, such as to: (a) back-up to some previous menu to change the selection made, (b) return to the main menu to restart the analysis, (c) enter a glossary to look up the definition of a term, (d) list all previous selections made along the way, and (e) quit.

Two additional features of the HAT are worth noting. One is that the HAT is capable of handling multiprinciple problems. For example, if the block in the problem in Fig. 5.2 were to experience a totally inelastic collision with a second block at the bottom of the ramp (i.e., the two blocks stick together after the collision), then the user could select Option 2 at the very last menu in order to return to the first menu and continue the "linear momentum" portion of the analysis. At the end of the analysis, the user would be provided with two sets of equations, namely the equations from the energy portion of the analysis (Menu 9

1

Which principle applies to this part of the problem solution?
  1. Newton's Second Law or Kinematics
  2. Angular Momentum
  3. Linear Momentum
  4. Work and Energy
Please enter your selection: [4]
(B)ackup (M)ain menu (G)lossary (L)ist selections (Q)uit

2

Describe the system in terms of its mechanical energy.
  1. Conservative system (conservation of energy)
  2. Non-conservative system
Please enter your selection: [1]
(B)ackup (M)ain menu (G)lossary (L)ist selections (Q)uit

3

Describe the changes in mechanical energy. Consider only the energy of one body at a time at some initial and final state.
  1. Change in kinetic energy
  2. Change in potential energy
  3. Change in potential and kinetic energy
Please enter your selection: [3]
(B)ackup (M)ain menu (G)lossary (L)ist selections (Q)uit

4

Describe the changes in kinetic energy.
  1. Change in translational kinetic energy
  2. Change in rotational kinetic energy
  3. Change in translational and rotational kinetic energies
Please enter your selection: [1]
(B)ackup (M)ain menu (G)lossary (L)ist selections (Q)uit

5

Describe the boundary conditions.
  1. No initial translational kinetic energy
  2. No final translational kinetic energy
  3. Initial and final translational kinetic energies
Please enter your selection: [1]
(B)ackup (M)ain menu (G)lossary (L)ist selections (Q)uit

6

Describe the changes in potential energy.
  1. Changes in gravitational potential energy
  2. Changes in spring potential energy
  3. Changes in gravitational and spring potential energy
Please enter your selection: [1]
(B)ackup (M)ain menu (G)lossary (L)ist selections (Q)uit

7

Describe the boundary conditions.
  1. No initial gravitational potential energy
  2. No final gravitational potential energy
  3. Initial and final gravitational potential energy
Please enter your selection: [2]
(B)ackup (M)ain menu (G)lossary (L)ist selections (Q)uit

8

Is there another body in the system which has not been examined?
  1. Yes
  2. No
Please enter your selection: [2]
(B)ackup (M)ain menu (G)lossary (L)ist selections (Q)uit

9

The Energy Principle states that the work done on the system by all non-conservative forces is equal to the change in the mechanical energy of the system:

$$W_{nc} = E_f - E_i$$

According to your selections,
$W_{nc} = 0$ (Conservative system: Mechanical energy is conserved)
$E_f = (1/2Mv^2)$ and $E_i = (Mgy)$
Please press any key to continue

10

Work and Energy
  1. Problem Solved
  2. Return to Main Menu to continue solution
  3. Review previous solution screens
Please enter your selection:

FIG. 5.1. HAT Analysis of Problem Shown in Fig. 5.2

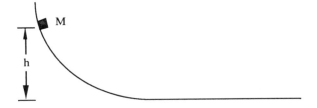

A small block of mass M slides along a track having both curved and horizontal sections as shown. If the particle is released from rest at height h, what is its speed when it is on the horizontal section of the track? The track is frictionless.

FIG. 5.2.   Sample Problem Analyzed by HAT Menus Shown in Fig. 5.1

in Fig. 5.1) and the equations resulting from the linear momentum portion of the analysis.

The second feature is that the HAT has the flexibility to accommodate problems that could be solved using two distinct methods. For example, a problem asking for the velocity of a falling object after it has descended a given height in the earth's gravitational field could be solved by selecting either "Work and Energy" or "Newton's Second Law or Kinematics" at the first menu. The selection of "Work and Energy" would lead to an analysis similar to that presented in Fig. 5.1. Choosing "Newton's Second Law or Kinematics" would put the user onto a path leading to the kinematic equations governing motion caused by a constant acceleration. If correct selections are made, both analyses would result in appropriate equations for solving the problem.

Description of Equation Sorting Tool (EST)

The EST is a sortable data base containing 178 equations taken from a standard classical mechanics textbook (Resnick & Halliday, 1977). Its design is consonant with novices' tendencies both to cue on surface features when deciding how to attack a problem and to focus their problem-solving efforts on finding and manipulating equations. Like the HAT, the EST neither tutors nor provides feedback to the user. Part of the motivation for implementing this environment on a computer was to have a second computer-based environment to use as a control treatment—that is, we needed to control for the possibility that simply using a computer may increase students' interest and motivation during treatment.

The EST data base can be sorted in three different ways: (a) by Problem Types, such as *inclined plane* and *falling bodies*, (b) by Variable Names, such as *mass* and *velocity*, and (c) by Physics Terms, such as *potential energy* and

Newton's Second Law. That is, the user can perform sequential sorts through the data base to reduce it to a small, manageable number of equations that might be useful for solving a problem (e.g., two sequential sorts using Problem Type *inclined plane* and Variable Name *velocity* will reduce the data base to those equations appropriate for inclined planes and containing the variable *v*). Basically the EST can be thought of as a lengthy "formula-sheet" that is cross-referenced and accessible via a large list of terms. These terms largely reflect the surface-feature terminology used by novices.

TWO STUDIES OF PROBLEM CATEGORIZATION

Some of the clearest differences in behavior between experts and novices have emerged from problem categorization experiments. When asked to categorize problems into groups, with the problems in each group related by the approach that would be used to solve them, experts tend to rely on the problems' *deep structure* (i.e., principles and concepts that could be applied to solve the problem) as the classification criterion (Chi et al., 1981; Glaser, chap. 4 in this volume; Hardiman, Dufresne, & Mestre, 1989; Schoenfeld & Herrmann, 1982). In contrast, novices tend to rely on the problems' surface features (i.e., objects and terminology described in the problems). Since the HAT highlights the importance of principles in problem solving, it is not unreasonable to expect that use of the HAT would promote shifts from surface-feature-based to deep-structure-based categorization. Two separate questions were investigated.

Do Hierarchical Problem Analyses Promote Categorization Based on Deep Structure?

To answer this question, we designed a categorization task that could evaluate the competing influence of deep structure and surface features in making categorization decisions. During this categorization task subjects were presented with a *model problem* and two *comparison problems* and asked to judge which of the two comparison problems would be solved most like the model problem. Comparison problems were constructed to match their corresponding model problem in one of four ways: (a) surface features, meaning that the objects and descriptor terms in the comparison problem matched those of the model problem, (b) deep structure, meaning that the same physical principle that could be applied to solve the comparison problem could also be applied to solve the model problem, (c) both surface features and deep structure, and (d) neither surface features nor deep structure. These four types of comparison problems were termed S, D, SD, and N, respectively.

Comparison problems were paired together such that one and only one comparison problem in each pair matched the model problem in deep structure. This

TABLE 5.1
Categorization Task: Sample Model Problem and Comparison Problems

Model problem:

A 2.5 kg ball or radius 4 cm is traveling at 7 m/s on a rough horizontal surface, but not spinning. Some distance later, the ball is rolling without slipping at 5 m/s. How much work was done by friction?

Surface feature (S) comparison problem:

A 3 kg soccer ball of radius 15 cm is initially sliding at 10 m/s without spinning. The ball travels on a rough horizontral surface and eventually rolls without slipping. Find the ball's final velocity.

Deep structure (D) comparison problem:

A small rock of mass 10 g falling vertically hits a very think layer of snow and penetrates 2 meters before coming to rest. If the rock's speed was 25 m/s just prior to hitting the snow, find the average force exerted on the rock by the snow.

Surface feature and deep structure (SD) comparison problem:

A .05 kg billiard ball of radius 2 cm rolls without slipping down an inclined plane. If the billiard ball is initially at rest, what is its speed after it has moved through a vertical distance of .5 m?

No (N) match comparison problem:

A 2 kg projectile is fired with an ititial volocity of 1500 m/s at an angle of 30 degrees above the horizontal and height 100 m above the ground. Find the time needed for the projectile to reach the ground.

constraint allowed the construction of four comparison problem pairings: (a) S-D, (b) S-SD, (c) N-D, and (d) N-SD. The task contained a total of 20 items. An example of five problems (model problem with S, D, SD, and N comparison problems) is given in Table 5.1. Further details on the task can be found elsewhere (Hardiman et al., 1989).

Assuming a novice-like categorization strategy based *strictly* on surface features, the following performance pattern was predicted: (a) S-D: 0% deep structure choices, (b) S-SD: 50% deep structure choices (both choices are equally "good" in terms of matching the model problem on surface features), (c) N-D: 50% deep structure choices (either alternative is equally "bad" in terms of matching the model problem on surface features), and (d) N-SD: 100% deep structure choices (a surface feature match to the model problem will also mean a deep structure match). On the other hand, an expert-like categorization strategy based *strictly* on deep structure would result in 100% deep structure choices for all four types. In reality, novices do not rely entirely on surface features and experts do not rely entirely on deep structure when making categorization decisions (Hardiman et al., 1989). Nevertheless, if a novice's categorization scheme becomes more expert-like, then we should observe a shift from surface-feature-based, to deep-structure-based categorizations.

The categorization task was administered prior to, and following treatment to 42 college subjects who volunteered to participate in the study. All subjects had

TABLE 5.2
Categorization Task: Percent Deep Structure Matches
(Study 1)

Group	Pretreatment Performance	Posttreatment Performance
HAT (N = 14)	56	66
EST (N = 14)	61	61
T (N = 14)	62	58
Total	60	62

finished a calculus-based, freshman-level classical mechanics course with a grade of B or better. These subjects were randomly divided into three groups, each undergoing a different treatment.

In all three treatments, subjects solved the same 25 problems, 5 at a time during hour-long sessions spread over 3 weeks. We refer to these 25 problems as the treatment problems. In the focal treatment, subjects used the HAT to solve the treatment problems. In one of the two control treatments, subjects used the EST to solve the treatment problems, whereas in the second control treatment subjects solved the treatment problems using the textbook from their mechanics course. The focal group and two control groups will be referred to as the HAT-group, the EST-group, and the T-group.

Table 5.2 shows the overall performance of the three treatment groups, where the entries indicate the percentage of deep structure matches. The HAT-group was the only group to show any increase in the number of deep structure matches following treatment. Although the improvement of the HAT-group was only 10 percentage points, this improvement was statistically significant and was the result of improvements across all four types of comparison problem pairings.

Is the Increase in Deep Structure Matches Due to an Increased Reliance on Principles?

Although HAT subjects showed an increase in the number of deep structure matches after treatment, the data did not allow us to determine whether this increase was actually due to a greater reliance on principle use when making categorization decisions. In order to determine the cause of the increase, we need to ascertain the reasoning underlying subjects' decisions. Therefore, another study was conducted using a similar procedure (i.e., a preassessment followed by treatment followed by a postassessment) but a different categorization task that allowed a determination of subjects' reasoning.

In the new categorization task, subjects were asked to decide whether or not pairs of problems would be solved similarly, and to state the reasons behind their decisions. Thus problems were paired together such that the pair shared one of the following attribute(s): (a) surface features (S), (b) deep structure (D), (c) both surface features and deep structure (SD), and (d) no similarity (N).

This task was administered prior to treatment to 44 new college volunteers who had earned a B or better in a calculus-based, freshman-level mechanics course. An examination of the preassessment results indicated that the reasons provided by subjects varied greatly. However, each subject could be classified as having a characteristic reasoning pattern. This situation provided the opportunity to explore whether or not novices displaying different reasoning patterns derived differential benefits from using the HAT. That is, use of the HAT might have a bigger impact on the categorization performance of novices who primarily used a surface-feature-based categorization scheme than on the performance of novices who already relied primarily on a deep-structure-based scheme.

The subjects were divided into three "reasoning groups" based on the type of reasoning they used the majority of the time on the categorization task administered prior to treatment. Those subjects who used surface-feature-based reasoning on more than half of the categorization items were placed in one group; those who used principle-based reasoning on the majority of the items were placed in a second group; those who used a mixture of strategies but no single strategy on more than half of the categorization items were placed in the third group. This partition resulted in 17 surface-feature reasoners, 11 principle-reasoners, and 16 mixed-reasoners.

We randomly selected 10 subjects from each of these three reasoning groups and divided the 30 into two treatment groups of 15 subjects each. Each reasoning group was equally represented in the two treatment groups. The focal treatment group used the HAT to solve 25 treatment problems, and will again be referred to as the "HAT-group." The control treatment group solved the treatment problems without the use of any external aid, and will be referred to as the "control (C)-group." Except for these changes, the experimental procedure was the same as that used in the previous study.

The decision to have the control group solve the treatment problems without the use of any external aid, such as the textbook or the EST was based on the results of the first study. There were several reasons for this decision. In the first study, subjects in the T-group made little use of the textbook in solving the treatment problems. Second, since the EST was designed to allow novices to search through equations using surface-feature terminology, use of the EST might encourage surface-feature-based categorization. Finally, the performance of the EST- and T-groups was nearly equivalent both prior to, and following treatment, suggesting that the type of control treatment used made little difference.

To evaluate the degree to which subjects relied on principles in making

TABLE 5.3
Categorization Task: Percent Principle Use
(Study 2)

Group	Preassessment	Postassessment
HAT (N = 15)	39	74
Control (N = 15)	33	56

categorization decisions, the pre- and postcategorization data were analyzed on the basis of whether principle-based reasoning was used on each item, regardless of whether or not the principle(s) used for judging solution similarity was appropriate. Thus, an item was awarded one point if a subject used principle-based reasoning and zero otherwise. On the precategorization task, both treatment groups performed similarly (see Table 5.3). However, significant performance differences emerged on the posttask with the HAT-group outperforming the C-group by 18 percentage points.

To ascertain whether or not there were differential improvements among the reasoning groups within the HAT-group, we analyzed the performance of the three reasoning groups separately. The surface-feature-reasoners and mixed-reasoners showed a large increase in principle use after the HAT treatment, but the principle-reasoners did not. The lack of a large improvement for the principle-reasoners was partially due to their ceiling-level performance both before and after treatment (78% prior to treatment vs. 83% following treatment); principle-reasoners simply had little room for improvement. *Because of this we will not discuss further the performance of principle-reasoners.* Rather, we will focus our attention on attempting to understand the nature of the gains made by surface-feature- and mixed-reasoners.

The combined performance of the surface-feature-reasoners and mixed-reasoners improved from 19% prior to treatment to 68% following treatment. Thus, it appears that subjects who were unlikely to make categorization decisions based on principles prior to treatment derived the most benefit from using the HAT. Indeed, the combined posttreatment performance of the surface-feature-reasoners and the mixed-reasoners at 68 was comparable to the pretreatment performance of the principle-reasoners from both the HAT-group (78) and the C-group (66).

The combined performance of the surface-feature-reasoners and mixed-reasoners for the C-group also showed some improvement. However, their 22 percentage point increase in principle-based reasoning (i.e., 16% prior to treatment and 38% following treatment) was much smaller than the 49 percentage point increase for the corresponding groups who used the HAT.

Although the data showed a greater *use* of principles among surface-feature-reasoners and mixed-reasoners, it does not necessarily follow that subjects were identifying *appropriate* principles for judging the similarity of solution of problem pairs. To investigate this issue, we analyzed the data of the surface-feature-reasoners and the mixed-reasoners based on whether the *correct* principle(s) was identified. An item was now awarded one point only if the principle(s) identified for judging whether or not the two problems would be solved similarly was correct, and zero otherwise.

The surface-feature-reasoners and the mixed-reasoners within the HAT-group showed more improvement on the total percentage of items in which correct principles were used to make the categorization decisions than did the corresponding reasoners in the control treatment. This result is statistically significant. For the HAT-group the combined performance of the surface-feature-reasoners and mixed-reasoners increased from 11% prior to treatment to 38% following treatment. For the C-group the increase went from 11% to 22%.

The fraction of the time that subjects selected a correct principle out of the total number of times they used principle-based reasoning was approximately the same both across the two treatment groups, and before and after treatment ($\frac{11}{19}$ = .58 prior to treatment vs. $\frac{38}{68}$ = .57 following treatment for the HAT treatment, compared to $\frac{11}{16}$ = .69 prior to treatment vs. $\frac{22}{38}$ = .58 following treatment for the C treatment). Although both groups increased the occasions of principle-based reasoning, the frequency with which they were able to determine the correct principle did not change. An alternative view is that subjects were able to identify the correct principle on the posttask in many situations where they had not used principle reasoning on the pretask.

Summary of the Two Categorization Studies

Taken together, the results from the two categorization studies suggest that structuring problem analyses to highlight the importance of principles increases novices' reliance on principles in making judgments of solution similarity. Further, the results provide some evidence that structured problem analyses increase novices' reliance on principles more than traditional forms of problem-solving activities. It would appear that these benefits can be fairly large for novices who are not predisposed to use principle-based reasoning.

Although the HAT treatment was fairly successful at increasing novices' use of principles, it had little effect on their accuracy in selecting correct principles. These results are not unexpected. Since the HAT highlighted the importance of principles by positioning the questions related to principle selection at the beginning of an analysis, HAT users were able to perceive the usefulness of principles in categorizing problems. However, the HAT does not instruct users on *how* to select principles correctly, and so there is no reason to expect that the accuracy with which one selects principles would improve as a result of using the HAT. It may be that direct instruction is needed to improve novices' accuracy in selecting a correct principle. Even so it is encouraging to observe that freshman students select principles when making categorization decisions with an accuracy of approximately 60%; thus increasing novices' reliance on principles is potentially a useful first step in getting novices to apply principles to solve problems.

It is less clear why novices in the control group of the second study showed any increase in principle-based reasoning after treatment. One possible explanation is that the act of problem solving itself impacts the way knowledge is structured in memory. This possibility is certainly consistent with the conventional wisdom that practice solving problems is the most important activity for training a novice. A more likely explanation, given that the treatment consisted of solving only 25 problems, is that a sizable portion of the gain by the control group is the result of reminding subjects of previous learning. This latter explanation is not in conflict with the lack of improvement in making deep structure matches displayed by the two control groups in the first study, since the categorization task used in that study did not permit the determination of the frequency of principle use.

STUDIES OF PROBLEM SOLVING

Problem-solving performance is considered the ultimate measure of expertise. This is because problem solving is a complex task involving the interplay of various cognitive factors (e.g., acquisition of a rich base of content knowledge, organization and retrieval of this knowledge, ability to identify what principles and procedures can be used to solve a problem, ability to execute a solution plan, and ability to evaluate both the solution plan and the answer for accuracy and reasonability). Since it takes years to become an expert problem solver, it is unlikely that any treatment of short duration will produce dramatic problem-solving improvements over a wide range of topics. Nevertheless, given the HAT's success at increasing principle use in problem categorization and the cognitive research findings (Hayes & Simon, 1976; Hinsley, Hayes, & Simon, 1977; Larkin, 1981; Newell & Simon, 1972; Simon & Simon, 1978) that indicate that categorization plays a major role in the problem-solving activities of experts, we explored the possibility that the HAT treatment would increase novices' problem-solving skills.

Do Hierarchical Analyses Improve Problem-Solving Performance?

An initial study (Mestre, Dufresne, Gerace, & Hardiman, 1988) comparing the relative effectiveness of the HAT, EST, and T treatments on improving problem-solving performance revealed that all three treatment groups achieved modest, indistinguishable levels of improvement as measured by pre- and postassessments of problem solving. In an attempt to understand the modest gains experienced by the HAT-group, we analyzed their performance on the 25 treatment problems by examining the key-strokes subjects made during the treatment sessions. The key-stroke data indicated that the HAT-group reached the *appropriate* equation screen (e.g., the equivalent of Menu 9 in Fig. 5.1) rather infrequently. Accordingly, the HAT-group's performance on the 25 treatment problems, as determined by the fraction of problems solved correctly, was approximately $\frac{1}{3}$. The rather low performance on the treatment problems suggests that subjects derived little, if any, benefit from using the HAT, at least in terms of ability to use the approach to solve problems.

A similar analysis of the performance of the two control groups on the treatment problems revealed only slightly higher levels of performance in comparison to the HAT-group. Upon closer scrutiny, it was determined that several treatment problems were so difficult that very few subjects from any of the treatment groups could solve them. Given the questionable value of using such difficult problems in the treatments, a new study was designed.

In the new problem-solving study, the set of 25 treatment problems used in the initial study was modified. The modification consisted of replacing 12 treatment problems that subjects found inordinately difficult in the initial study with 12 new treatment problems of moderate difficulty; these new treatment problems covered the same topics as the original 12. The 13 treatment problems from the initial study that were of moderate difficulty were kept for the new study. This change was intended to enhance the chances that subjects would be able to obtain correct solutions. With regard to the HAT-group, we believed that making the treatment problems easier would help subjects focus their attention on using the HAT rather than on being intimidated by the problems' level of difficulty. We hypothesized that if subjects became more successful at using the HAT then they would perceive the value of the approach for solving problems, and would thereby exhibit greater improvement on problem-solving measures.

The subjects and experimental procedure used in the new problem-solving study were the same as those used in the second categorization study where the HAT treatment was compared to the C treatment (the new set of 25 treatment problems was also used in the second categorization study). Problem-solving performance prior to and following treatment were assessed with two equivalent test forms. Each test form contained four problems, one each requiring the application of Newton's Laws, energy principles, momentum principles, and angular momentum principles. The order in which the two forms were administered was randomized, with a particular subject receiving one test form as the preassessment and the other as the postassessment. The assessments were graded independently by two physicists in a style similar to that which would be used to

TABLE 5.4
Problem-Solving Task: Score out of 100

Group	Pretest	Posttest
HAT (N = 15)	35.0	88.0
Control (N = 15)	39.8	76.5

grade a final exam. Each problem was graded on a basis of 10 points; if discrepancies of more than 1 point emerged in the grading of a problem, the solution was reevaluated and a grade was determined by consensus.

Table 5.4 contains the pre- and postassessment results, with entries denoting percent correct. The overall improvement achieved by the HAT-group was greater than that achieved by the C-group. This result is statistically significant. Further, all three reasoning groups using the HAT showed greater improvements than the corresponding reasoning groups receiving the control treatment.

The performance data on the treatment problems is shown in Table 5.5; the first column contains the corresponding data for the preliminary problem-solving study and the second column contains the data for the redesigned study. Reducing the level of difficulty of the treatment problems resulted in a higher percent correct for the HAT-group on the treatment problems in comparison to the C-group, as well as to both the HAT and the two control groups combined (EST and T) from the preliminary study.

Discussion of Problem-Solving Studies

The results from the second problem-solving study suggest that qualitative and hierarchically structured problem analyses can improve problem-solving performance more than student-directed problem-solving activities. However, the fact that both treatment groups showed a significant improvement in problem-solving performance implies that much of the improvement derives simply from engag-

TABLE 5.5
Performance on Treatment Problems: Percentage of Correct Answers

Group(s)	First Study	Second Study
HAT	34 (N = 14)	59 (N = 15)
Control	43 (N = 28)	43 (N = 15)

ing in problem-solving activities. What fraction of this improvement reflects new learning and what fraction reflects remindings of previous learning is unclear. In any case, differences in posttest performance between the two treatment groups can be interpreted as a consequence of the different problem-solving approaches used in the two treatments.

Taken together, the results from the two problem-solving studies seem to imply that for the HAT approach to be of value for improving novices' problem-solving skills over and beyond any improvements achieved by traditional approaches, novices must be able to use the approach to solve treatment problems with some degree of proficiency. During the first study, although the HAT-group only improved on the problem-solving test by an amount similar to that obtained by the control groups, this result was observed following a treatment phase during which the HAT group was only able to solve correctly 34% of the treatment problems. During the second study, in which the HAT-group (made up of a new group of students) correctly solved 59% of the treatment problems, the HAT-group showed more improvement on the problem-solving task than did the control group.

When comparing the percentage of correctly solved treatment problems from the first study with the percentage correct from the second study, it must be kept in mind that the second study used easier treatment problems. Thus, the greater percentage of treatment problems solved correctly during the second study does not imply that the HAT subjects used in the second study were better problem solvers or better at using the HAT than were the HAT subjects used in the first study. Generally, one must be cautious of conclusions drawn from comparisons of groups from different studies since these groups are not experimentally matched. Nevertheless, we believe it is safe to assume that novices must be able to use the HAT with some degree of success before they can apply the approach implicit in the HAT to solve problems on their own.

GENERAL DISCUSSION OF EXPERIMENTAL FINDINGS

At this point we would like to speculate on the mechanism by which the HAT treatment produced the observed differential improvements in performance when compared to the control treatments. It is clear that the complex structure of the HAT, combined with the short duration of the treatment and the lack of coaching and feedback, make it nearly impossible for novices to learn to reproduce the various solution paths. Any explanation of how the HAT induced the behavioral changes must take into account the knowledge base of novices. After completing an introductory course in mechanics novices will possess a moderate amount of quantitative knowledge (e.g., equations, relationships, and standard computational operations such as finding the magnitude of a vector). However, research consistently indicates that it is highly unlikely that novices will have made appropriate connections between quantitative knowledge and conceptual knowledge (Sweller, 1988). Our findings suggest that by stressing the relationship between principles, procedures, and equations, the HAT helped novices begin to integrate conceptual knowledge and quantitative knowledge within a problem-solving context. We believe that it was this integration that manifested itself in the shifts toward more principle-based reasoning in the various problem-solving tasks assessed.

Two additional factors contribute to the aforementioned conclusions. An associated study (Touger, Dufresne, Gerace, & Mestre, 1987) that examined students' explanations of physical phenomena revealed an increased use of principles after the HAT treatment. In contrast, the two control treatments used in this study (EST and T) actually decreased subjects' reliance on principles. The increased reliance on principles by the HAT group in the explanations task is consistent with the findings reported here. However, we can only conjecture that the decrease in principle use exhibited in the explanations task by the two control groups may have been due to the recent practice of formulaic problem-solving approaches during treatment.

Another indication that the HAT subjects recognized the value of principles for problem solving was found in their written responses to attitudinal questions from a questionnaire administered at the end of the study. Two sample responses from HAT subjects are:

- "It [the HAT] is useful in that it requires a systematic approach to problem solving—develops good habits. This method exposes the fundamental principles involved in each problem. This is very instructive."
- "It made you think about the kinds of basic laws you'd be using. Also, it forced you to classify each type of problem."

In contrast, EST users often remarked on the usefulness of having lots of equations readily available, thereby indicating that the EST may have actually reinforced their tendency toward a formulaic approach.

In summary, the studies reported herein suggest that in the near future we will be able to design instructional strategies that facilitate the acquisition of the kind of problem-solving behavior that we strive to teach students. How to design an instructional program to promote skilled problem solving with maximum efficiency remains an open question, as we hope to illustrate in the discussion contained in following section.

DIRECTIONS FOR FUTURE RESEARCH

The findings that emerged from the research we have reported, as well as from the research of other groups, are the result of carefully controlled experiments. Most problem-solving studies pose focused, well-defined questions and have a carefully controlled procedure for answering these questions. The classroom, however, is a different world from the microcosm in which carefully controlled experiments are conducted. We know a lot about the nature of expertise, but we know little about how to apply this knowledge to help an individual move along the road to expertise more efficiently. For example, we can describe fairly accurately the different stages through which an individual passes while becoming an expert in terms of measurable performance on various cognitive tasks. However, we know very little about how to integrate our knowledge about expertise into the design of coherent instructional packages for use in the classroom.

The research we have presented shows that it is possible to promote behavior in physics novices that reflects behavior observed in experts with a short treatment that contained no tutorial features. Yet even within this narrow context we know little about how to design the most efficient method for applying these findings within the context of instruction. How do we design an effective instructional environment that has the HAT approach at its core? Is the HAT approach too rigid an approach to impose on students because it leaves them with too little freedom to experiment with their own problem-solving style? Is the HAT approach only useful after a student has gone through a course and has acquired a modest amount of requisite knowledge, or can the approach be used effectively from the beginning of a course? What other kind of instructional support and strategies (e.g., consistent presentation of conceptual and quantitative knowledge in a hierarchical format and continued integration of all knowledge into a cohesive pyramidal structure; collaborative learning and problem solving among small groups of students) would enhance the development of skilled problem-solving behavior? These are important questions to answer if we are to develop a curriculum designed to facilitate the acquisition and retention of domain knowledge and the efficient use of this knowledge to solve problems.

When exploring uncharted research questions, especially those that have a direct bearing on curriculum design, whether in physics or other domains, we must be willing to be patient and to take risks. For example, it is quite conceivable that the most efficient way of promoting skilled behavior across several disciplines (e.g., mathematics, science, and writing) would be with a multiyear, sustained instructional effort in which we would measure little progress in the early stages but considerable progress during the late stages. If this were the case, convincing school administrators, teachers and parents that such a curriculum should be adopted would be a formidable task. We seem to demand that our educational system produce measurable results quickly, even if the "results" reflect that students are able to remember and recite back factual information, rather than solve complex problems.

IMPLICATIONS FOR LEARNING AND INSTRUCTION

Despite the many unanswered questions raised in the previous section, cognitive research has reached a level of maturity where we can begin to apply research findings in the design of classroom-based instructional strategies. What immediate implications do our findings have for classroom instruction in physics? Our findings indicate that, at least for students who have some prior knowledge of the subject matter, qualitative and hierarchically structured problem analyses can enhance the appreciation of the role of principles for problem solving. Further, these findings suggest that structured problem-solving activities that integrate conceptual knowledge with procedural knowledge are a more efficient means for promoting expertise than are student-directed problem-solving activities. This view is consistent with the results of other studies (Larkin, 1981, 1983; Larkin et al., 1980b; Simon & Simon, 1978; Sweller, 1988).

In quantitative domains, such as physics, there are various ways in which an instructor can encourage the use of principles within a classroom setting. A problem categorization task could be used not only to diagnose the extent to which students are cuing on problems' surface features, but also as a springboard for classroom discussions on how to go about extracting the deep structure from a problem's storyline. Asking students to perform qualitative analyses of problems and posing "what if" physical situations without resorting to writing equations can be used to ascertain students' ability to draw on concepts to explain physical phenomena, and to promote classroom discussions on the role of principles and qualitative analyses in problem solving. Yet another activity that would encourage the integration of qualitative and quantitative approaches is to ask students first to write down a qualitative solution plan for a problem involving the principles and procedures that could be applied, and then to instantiate the plan. In short, any activity where students actively participate in using principles as global "themes" and in tethering related information to these themes should help students structure their knowledge into cohesive chunks that are conducive for the effective recall and use of the knowledge in problem-solving situations.

Finally, we would like to assert that we are not advocating the abolition of conventional problem-solving activities as a means of promoting expertise. Conventional, student-directed problem-solving activities help novices become familiar with many useful relationships and make abstract knowledge operational. However, once the knowledge base is sufficiently developed, it becomes important to help the novice structure this knowledge for its efficient use in problem-solving settings. It is in the development of hierarchical knowledge structures and in the integration of conceptual and procedural knowledge that conventional problem-solving activities are lacking and structured activities are effective.

ACKNOWLEDGMENTS

Work supported by National Science Foundation grant BNS-8511069. The contents herein do not necessarily reflect the position, policy, or endorsement of NSF.

6 Teaching of Thinking Skills in the Sciences and Mathematics

Richard E. Mayer
University of California, Santa Barbara

What does it mean to teach for thinking? Can the way that we teach affect the way that our students think? Can education help students to improve their thinking; if so, how and how much? These are the kinds of questions that motivate this chapter.

My purpose here is to explore the idea that students can be taught in ways that help them become better thinkers. By better thinkers I mean students who are better able to take what they have learned and successfully use it in new situations. These students are better able to transfer knowledge about solving problems to new problems that they were not taught about.

In particular, I examine three exemplary thinking skills programs carried out through our research laboratory in Santa Barbara that demonstrate techniques for improving students' thinking skills in the domains of scientific thinking, mathematical thinking, and computer programing, respectively. In *structure training*, students learn how to outline sections of their science textbooks based on typical ways of organizing scientific text. In *representation training*, students learn how to translate sentences from mathematical word problems into concrete diagrams. In *conceptual model training*, students learn how to describe what goes on inside the computer for several BASIC computer programing statements. Each training program results in improvements in students' abilities to transfer what they had learned to new problem-solving tasks. These successful programs of teaching for thinking are based on teaching small, component skills rather than viewing intellectual performance as based on a single, monolithic ability; asking students to model the process of problem solving rather than only to produce the correct answer; and embedding instruction within specific subject matter domains rather than isolating thinking instruction as a separate domain-free topic.

95

WHAT IS TEACHING FOR THINKING?

Suppose we ask a student to read a passage about hearing such as summarized in the top left portion of Table 6.1. Then, we ask the student to answer retention questions that focus on material that was explicitly presented in the passage and transfer questions that require the student to creatively apply what was presented to new situations. For example, the middle portion of the first row of Table 6.1 lists a retention problem and the right top portion of Table 6.1 lists a transfer problem based on the hearing passage.

Next, suppose we teach a student to solve two-step word problems such as shown in the left portion of the second row in Table 6.1. Following instruction, we test the student on retention problems that are very similar to those given during instruction such as other similarly worded two-step problems and on transfer problems that go beyond what was explicitly taught such as three-step problems. Examples are shown in the middle and right portions of the second row in Table 6.1, respectively.

Finally, suppose we teach a student to generate and comprehend each of 10 elementary BASIC programing statements such as INPUT, LET, PRINT, and so on. Following instruction, we test the student on retention problems that are very similar to those given during instruction such as generating single statements and on transfer problems such as generating and comprehending short programs that go beyond what was explicitly taught. Examples of taught material, retention questions, and transfer questions are shown in the left, middle, and right portions of the third row of Table 6.1, respectively.

Table 6.2 lists three possible learning outcomes for any of these examples. First, the student may perform poorly on retention and on transfer. This performance would suggest that the student did not learn very much—labeled *no learning* in Table 6.2. Second, the student may perform well on retention but poorly on transfer. This student would seem to have learned what was taught but be unable to apply what has been learned in new situations. In Table 6.2, this kind of learning outcome is labeled *nonmeaningful learning*. Finally, the student may perform well on retention and on transfer, indicating that the student learned the material and was able to apply what was learned to new situations. Table 6.2 refers to this outcome as *meaningful learning* (Mayer, 1987c).

The analysis summarized in Table 6.2 is intended only as an illustration that requires a great deal of additional research and theory-based clarification. However, it does provide a simple way of defining meaningful learning, namely meaningful learning is learning that results in transfer of learned material to new situations. The goal of teaching for thinking is to create meaningful learning, the third kind of learning outcome listed in Table 6.2. For purposes of this chapter, teaching for thinking can be defined as an attempt to teach domain specific material in a way that enables students to use what they learn to solve transfer problems.

TABLE 6.1
Examples of Retention and Transfer Problems in Three Subject Matter Domains

Taught Material	Retention Problem	Transfer Problem
Hearing can be described in five separate stages. First sound waves are captured by the external portion of the ear. The outer ear's function is to focus or concentrate these sound waves. During the second stage, the sound waves travel down the auditory canal (a tube embedded in the bones of the skull)...	A tube embedded in the bones of the skull is called _____.	A child cannot hear sound in her left ear. List as many possible reasons as you can think of.
Tom is 35 years old. Zino is 7 years older than Tom. How old will Zino be in 10 years?	Mary is 12 years old. Her sister is 6 years older than her. How old will Mary's sister be in 2 years?	Alfredo is 25 years old. Pedro is 7 years younger than Alfredo and Dennis is 3 years older than Pedro. How old will Dennis be in 8 years?
Assume that you type in Let A = 1 and press the RETURN key. The value, 1, will be stored in variable A. Assume that you type in LET B = 2 and press the RETURN key. The value, 2, will be stored in variable B. Finally, assume that you type in LET C = A + B and press the RETURN key. The value, 3, will be stored in variable C...	Which of the following is not a legal statement? LET A = 1 LET B = 2 LET A + B = C	What number will appear on the screen after you run the following program? LET X = 5 LET Y = X LET Y = X + Y PRINT

97

TABLE 6.2
Three Possible Learning Outcomes

Type of Outcome	Retention Performance	Transfer Performance
No learning	poor	poor
Nonmeaningful learning	good	poor
Meaningful learning	good	good

HOW CAN WE TEACH FOR THINKING?

As an introduction to the issues involved in teaching for thinking, let me ask you to imagine that you were responsible for developing an educational program that would improve the way that students think. Assume that you have vast economic resources and commitments from the nation's school systems to faithfully implement your program. What would you do?

If you took the time to consult the research literature you would find that previous attempts to teach students to become better thinkers have not always turned out to be well-documented successes (Detterman & Sternberg, 1982; Mayer, 1987a, 1987b; Nickerson, Perkins, & Smith, 1985; Segal, Chipman, & Glaser, 1985). From the Latin School movement's attempts to teach "proper habits of mind" in previous centuries to more modern attempts to stimulate cognitive development through Project Head Start, the search for solid evidence of teaching students to think has been elusive and often disappointing (Mayer, 1987a, 1987b). In fact, one of the most persistent research findings in the problem-solving literature is that people who learn how to solve one kind of problem rarely are able to transfer what they learned to solving new kinds of problems (Mayer, 1983).

In spite of this disappointing history, however, current research and theory in cognitive psychology may hold some answers that were not available for previous thinking skills projects. In particular, in order to develop a program of teaching for thinking there are several questions you would need to answer concerning what should be taught, how it should be taught, and where it should be taught. These issues are summarized in Table 6.3.

The first question is what should be taught: Should we view thinking as a single, unitary intellectual ability or as a collection of smaller, component skills? The course taken in this chapter is to view the content of a problem-solving program as a collection of small, component skills such as techniques for how to outline scientific text, how to represent sentences from story problems in diagram form, or how to relate lines of computer programing code to a concrete model of the computer.

TABLE 6.3
Three Issues Underlying Teaching for Thinking

Issue	Alternatives
1. What to teach	Thinking as a single intellecutal ability *versus* thinking as a collection of smaller component skills.
2. How to teach	Focus on product through rewarding correct answers *versus* focus on processes that the student learns to model.
3. Where to teach	In general, domain-independent courses *versus* within existing, specific subject matter areas.

The second question concerns how to teach: Should we focus on product or process, that is, on getting the right answers in problem solving or on the methods and strategies for problem solving? This report opts for the second approach such as helping students to model the process by which an expert thinks about solving scientific, mathematical, or programing problems.

The third question focuses on where thinking should be taught: Is it better to teach thinking skills in domain-independent, general problem-solving courses or to integrate thinking skills instruction within existing subject-material domains? The research literature on transfer of problem-solving skills prompts me to focus on the second option. Instead of examining teaching of general thinking skills, this chapter examines teaching for thinking within three specific domains: science, mathematics, and computer programing.

In summary, a comparison of the features of successful and unsuccessful (or undocumented) thinking skills programs suggests three conditions for success: a focus on teaching component skills, use of modeling techniques that emphasize problem-solving process, and embedding instruction within existing subject matter domains (Mayer, 1987a, 1987b).

TEACHING FOR SCIENTIFIC THINKING

Issue

As an example, consider the following scenario. Some students are taking their first college science course at a junior college. The students are relatively inexperienced in reading college-level science textbooks and lack strong backgrounds in science. They devote a great deal of time and energy to the course, including reading every word of their textbooks. However, when the teacher posts the examination grades it is clear that the students are not passing the course. In particular, some students are often able to remember facts from the textbook but they have difficulty in applying the information from their textbooks to solve new problems; other students even have difficulty in remembering facts from the textbook.

What is your diagnosis? Based on the analysis given in Table 6.2, the students appear to have acquired learning outcomes that correspond to *no learning* or *nonmeaningful learning*. The students may have excellent strategies for reading narrative text but seem to lack appropriate strategies for reading expository text. What is your prescription for remediating this problem? What we need is a method of teaching the students to read their science textbooks in a way that results in meaningful learning—that is, in a way that allows them to transfer what they have learned to new problems.

Structure Training

What can we do to help science students become more effective learners and thinkers? Cook (1982; Cook & Mayer, 1988) devised a structure training program to help students improve their comprehension of scientific text. The training takes about 9 hours and consists of two major objectives. The first objective is to teach students how to distinguish among various text structures commonly found in science text. In Table 6.4, several of the text structures often used in science textbooks, including generalization, enumeration, and sequence are described and exemplified. When given a paragraph from their own science textbook, students learn to identify its text structure.

The second objective is to teach students how to outline passages of each type of text structure. For example, for generalization passages students write the main assertion followed by the supporting evidence; for sequence, they name and describe each step in the process; for enumeration, they list the main topic and subtopics. The worksheet that students use to learn about outlining generalization passages is summarized in Table 6.5.

Each session involves several episodes of presenting students with a paragraph from their own textbook, asking students to identify the paragraph's text structure, and then asking students to outline the paragraph. Students receive practice with feedback, and the instructor serves as a model for how to identify and outline paragraphs.

As you can see, Cook's structure training is consistent with the three aspects of successful programs described in the first section of this chapter. First, the training focuses on small, component skills—namely, strategies for how to recognize and outline specific kinds of text structures. Second, the training emphasizes process—namely, active modeling of reading comprehension techniques. Third, the training is embedded within a specific subject matter area—namely, reading science textbooks.

TABLE 6.4
Examples of Text Structures Used in Science Textbooks

GENERALIZATION

Description: Passage always has a main idea. Most of the other sentences in the passage try to provide evidence for the main idea by either clarifying or extending. Some sentences explain the main idea by using examples or illustrations; these tend to clarify the main idea. Other sentences explain the main idea in more detail; these extend the main idea.

Example: Irritability is defined as an organism's capacity to respond to conditions outside itself. An organism responds to a stimulus from the environment. The stimulus may be light, temperture, water, sound, the presence of a chemical substance, or a threat to life. The organism's response is the way it reacts to stimulus. For example, a plant may have a growth response. This happens when a root pushes toward water or a stem grown unevenly and bends toward light.

ENUMERATION

Description: List of facts one after another. There are two general kinds of enumeration passages: Specified—actually lists the facts by by numbering them; unspecified—lists facts in paragraph form, with each fact stated in one or more sentences.

Example: There are four general properties of solids: (1) Tenacity is a measure of a solid's resistance to being pulled apart. (2) Hardness is a measure of a substance's ability to scratch another substance. (3) Malleability refers to a solid's ability to be hammered or rolled into thin sheets. (4). Ductility is the ability to be drawn out in the form of wires.

SEQUENCE

Description: Describe a continuous and connected series of events or the steps in a process. Examples of sequences include changes as the result of growth, a biological process, steps in an experiment or the evolution of some event.

Example: Hearing can be described in five separate stages. First, sound waves are captured by the external portion of the ear. The outer ear's function is to focus or concentrate these sound waves. During the second stage, the sound waves travel down the auditory canal (a tude embedded in the bones of the skull) and strike the tympanic membrane or eardrum. The third stage occurs when the vibrations of the eardrum begin a series of similar vibrations in several small bones. These vibrations are then transmitted to the inner ear called the cochlea during the fourth stage. At this point the vibrations are turned into neural impulses that are sent to the brain. The fifth and final stage of the hearing process represents the brain's interpretation of the sound patterns.

Evaluation of Structure Training

Does structure training work? To answer this question, Cook provided structure training to a group of introductory chemistry students at a junior college. Before training, the students took a pretest in which they read biology passages and then were asked to recall and answer questions about the passages. After training, the students took an equivalent posttest. Control students from the same course took the pretest and posttest without training during the intervening period.

The pretest-to-posttest changes in recall and question-answering performance of the structure trained and control groups are summarized in Fig. 6.1. For the pretest, both groups scored at about the same level for each measure of perfor-

TABLE 6.5
Example Worksheet for Structure Training

Step One:	Identify the generalization (main idea). List and define key words in the generalization.

WORD   DEFINITION

Restate the generalization in your own words

Step Two:	What kind of support is there for the generalization? Does it use examples, illustrations? Does it extend or clarify the gneralization?

SUPPORTING EVIDENCE   RELATION TO GENERALIZATION

Note. This worksheet is for generalization passages.

mance: recalling important information, recalling unimportant information, correctly answering retention questions, and correctly answering transfer questions. However, as you can see in Fig. 6.1, the trained group showed a large pretest-to-posttest gain in recalling important information and answering transfer questions whereas the control group did not.

These results are consistent with the idea that structure training helped students focus on the important information in their textbooks and to organize the information in a way that allowed for successful transfer. The pattern of performance of the trained group is consistent with the description of meaningful learning outcomes as presented in the introduction, whereas the control group's performance more closely corresponds to nonmeaningful learning.

Although the results were positive, it is important to note the conditions under which the results were achieved. First, if we had focused only on overall amount recalled or overall amount retained, we would not have concluded that structure training had an effect. The effects of structure training are most obvious when we look at transfer performance and at recall of important information. Second, if our subjects had been experienced readers of scientific text, our instructional training probably would not have been successful. This is so because experienced science readers are likely to have already developed appropriate reading comprehension strategies. The effects of structure training are likely to be most pronounced for students who are adequate readers but who lack domain-specific experience in reading scientific text.

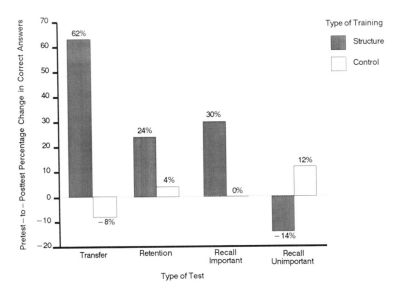

FIG. 6.1.   Pretest-to-posttest changes of structure-trained and control · groups.

TEACHING FOR MATHEMATICAL THINKING

Issue

As a second example, suppose we walked into a mathematics classroom and asked the students to solve some problems like those in Table 6.6. These are called two-step problems because each problem requires two mathematical computations, such as adding .05 to 1.13 and multiplying the result by 5. The problem on the top is called *consistent* because the key word in the problem (i.e., *more*) is consistent with the required arithmetic operation (i.e., addition) whereas the problem on the bottom is called *inconsistent* because the key word in the problem (i.e., *less*) conflicts with the required operation (i.e., addition).

Although both problems require the same arithmetic operations, suppose we find that students are far more likely to make errors on the inconsistent problems than consistent problems. A particularly difficult aspect of these problems is that they contain relational statements, that is, sentences that assert a quantitative relationship between two variables such as the second sentence in each problem in Table 6.6 (Mayer, 1982). For example, instead of adding 1.13 and .05 in the second problem, a sizeable proportion of students subtract .05 from 1.13. Even though our students can solve computational problems such as $(1.13 + .05) \times 5 = \underline{\hspace{1cm}}$, they are often unable to solve corresponding word problems such as the

TABLE 6.6
Examples of Word Problems Used in Mathematics Education

Consistent Two-Step

At ARCO gas sells for $1.13 per gallon. Gas at Chevron is 5 cents more per gallon than gas at ARCO. How much do 5 gallons of gas cost at Chevron?

Inconsistent Two-Step Program

At ARCO, gas sells for $1.13 per gallon. This is 5 cents less per gallon than gas at Chevron. How much do 5 gallons of gas cost at Chevron?

---

second problem in Table 6.6. This pattern of performance was obtained in a study by Lewis and Mayer (1987).

What are the kinds of knowledge that our students need in order to solve word problems like the gasoline problem in Table 6.6? Table 6.7 provides a summary of how mathematical problem solving can be broken down into two major phases: representation, in which the student creates a mental representation of the problem; and solution, in which the student establishes and carries out a plan for appropriate mathematical operations such as addition and multiplication (Mayer, 1985a; Mayer, Larkin, & Kadane, 1984). For example, in the gasoline problem, problem representation involves translating each sentence into other forms such as diagrams or equations and then integrating this information into a coherent representation; problem solution involves devising a plan such as finding the cost

TABLE 6.7
Types of Knowledge Required to Solve Word Problems

Problem: At ARCO gas sells for $1.13 per gallon. This is 5 cents less per gallon than gas at Chevron. How much do 5 gallons of gas cost at Chevron?

Step	Knowledge	Examples from Gasoline Problem
Representation		
	Linguistic:	"Gas" and "gasoline" refer to the same thing
	Factual:	There are 100 cents in a dollar.
	Schematic:	This is a comparison problem.
Solution		
	Strategic:	The goals are to find the cost per gallon at Chevron and the total cost of gas at Chevron.
	Procedural:	Add .05 to 1.13; multiply 1.18 by 5

---

per gallon and then finding the total cost, and executing the plan by adding .05 and 1.13 and then multiplying 1.18 by 5.

What is your diagnosis concerning our students' knowledge for mathematical problem solving? It appears that the students are having difficulty in the representation of word problems, because the wording of the problem seems to be a major factor in eliciting errors. What can be done to improve students' mathematical problem-solving performance? A straightforward implication is that some students may need training in how to represent the sentences of word problems. In particular, students need practice in how to represent relational statements such as, "This is 5 cents less per gallon than gas at Chevron." This recommendation is particularly important in light of the observation that most mathematics textbooks emphasize problem solution whereas students' major difficulties occur in problem representation.

Representation Training

Lewis (1989a, 1989b) developed a 2-hour training program to help students improve their problem-representation skills for mathematical problem solving. Students learn to identify relational statements and to translate relational statements into diagrams using a number line. For example, the worksheet in Table 6.8 shows the procedure that students learn for translating sentences into diagrams. As you can see, the student receives practice in systematically translating sentences into diagrams rather than relying on key words such as *more* or *less*.

Like Cook's (1982) structure training, Lewis's representation training is consistent with each of the three characteristics of successful problem-solving programs described in the introduction of this chapter. Representation training focuses on small, component skills—namely strategies for how to recognize and represent relational statements. Further, representation training relies on students learning to model the appropriate process—systematically translating sentences into diagrams. Finally, the training is part of a specific subject matter domain—solving word problems.

Evaluation of Representation Training

What are the effects of representation training? To answer this question, Lewis provided representation training to a group of college students who had trouble solving word problems. Before training, the students took a pretest that included two-step word problems like those shown in Table 6.6 as well as word problems that required three arithmetic steps, such as:

Alfredo is 25 years old. He is 7 years younger than Pedro who is 3 years older than Dennis. How old will Dennis be in 8 years?

TABLE 6.8
Example Worksheet for Representation Training

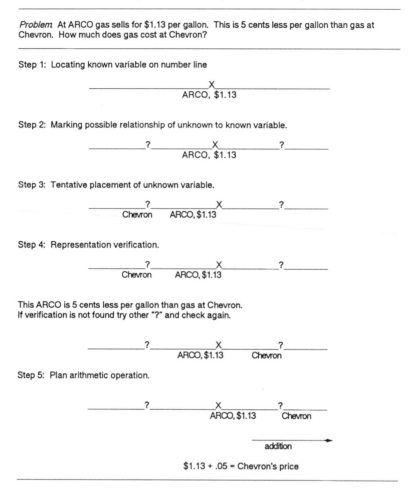

Problem At ARCO gas sells for $1.13 per gallon. This is 5 cents less per gallon than gas at Chevron. How much does gas cost at Chevron?

Step 1: Locating known variable on number line

Step 2: Marking possible relationship of unknown to known variable.

Step 3: Tentative placement of unknown variable.

Step 4: Representation verification.

This ARCO is 5 cents less per gallon than gas at Chevron.
If verification is not found try other "?" and check again.

Step 5: Plan arithmetic operation.

$1.13 + .05 = Chevron's price

After training, students took a posttest that included equivalent two-step and three-step word problems. A control group received practice in solving the same problems that the trained group solved but without any direction in how to represent problems. In both groups, the example problems required one or two steps but not three steps, so two-step problems can be considered as retention problems and three-step problems can be considered as transfer problems.

The bar graph in Fig. 6.2 summarizes the pretest-to-postest changes in error rates on solving two-step (retention) and three-step (transfer) word problems for the trained and control groups. For two-step (retention) problems, both groups

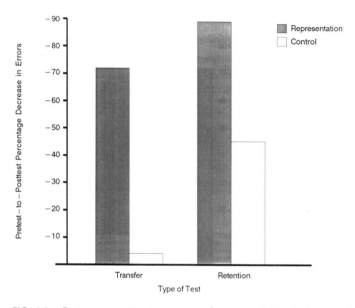

FIG. 6.2. Pretest-to-posttest changes of representation-trained and control groups.

averaged about the same number of errors on the pretest. Both groups showed a pretest-to-posttest improvement in solving two-step problems although the trained group improved significantly more than the control group. For three-step (transfer) problems, both groups averaged about the same number of errors on the pretest. However, on the posttest, the trained group showed significant improvement in solving transfer problems whereas the control group did not. The findings can be summarized by saying that the trained group displayed evidence of transfer to three-step problems whereas the control group did not.

These results demonstrate that representation training can improve students' creative problem-solving transfer performance. Even though students were trained on two-step problems they were able to transfer what they had learned to a new problem situation, namely three-step problems. The trained group's ability to transfer is consistent with the definition of meaningful learning outcomes described in the introduction. Apparently, representation training is another example of teaching for thinking.

The effectiveness of representation training may be limited by the characteristics of the learners. For example, the students in Lewis's study possessed good computational skills and good reading skills. If the students had not possessed these skills, it is unlikely that a small amount of representation training would have helped them. Similarly, although the students possessed good arithmetic and reading skills, they lacked experience in solving arithmetic word problems.

If the students were already expert problem solvers, representation training would not have been needed for them. In short, representation training is likely to be most valuable for students who possess appropriate background skills in computation but who perform poorly on solving word problems.

TEACHING FOR THINKING IN COMPUTER PROGRAMING

Issue

As a third example, suppose that students who have never had any experience in computer programing or high-level mathematics are given the opportunity to learn BASIC computer programing. Furthermore, assume that they participate in three sessions in which they read a standard BASIC manual and have hands-on experience with computers. In the training, they learn to use statements such as READ, DATA, INPUT, LET, PRINT, GOTO, IF, FOR, NEXT, and END.

When we test students on retention, such as writing grammatically correct statements or answering questions about simple facts from the manual, they perform well. For example, they are able to fill in the correct answer for the problem, "The computer will execute the statement following THEN only when the statement immediately following ____ is true." (The correct answer is "IF.") When we test our students on transfer, such as writing or comprehending short programs, they perform poorly. For example, they have difficulty explaining what the following program does:

```
10  INPUT A, B, C
20  LET D = A + B + C
30  D = D/3
40  PRINT D
50  END
```

This pattern of results was obtained in several studies (Bayman & Mayer, 1983, 1988).

What do students need to know in order to perform well on solving programing problems? Mayer (1988a) has identified four kinds of knowledge that may be required for successful problem solving in programing: syntactic, semantic, schematic, and strategic knowledge. Syntactic knowledge refers to knowledge of language features and facts such as knowing that each line in a BASIC program must begin with a line number. Semantic knowledge (Mayer, 1985b) refers to a conceptual model of the computer system including the kinds of actions that can take place inside the computer (e.g., moving, erasing, copying), the kinds of locations in the computer (e.g., input queue, output screen, memory space), and the kinds of objects that can be acted on (e.g., numbers, program lines, pointers). Schematic knowledge refers to knowledge of program modules that carry out specific functions such as modules for sorting data or for ordering data. Strategic knowledge refers to techniques for using syntactic, semantic, and schematic knowledge to develop and execute solution plans.

Because the students are in the preliminary phases of learning BASIC, we will focus only on their acquisition of syntactic and semantic knowledge as summarized in Table 6.9. It appears from the students' performance that they can retain the syntactic information from the manual but they have difficulty in transfering what they have learned to solving new problems. A straightforward diagnosis of their problem is that they have acquired syntactic knowledge but have not acquired appropriate semantic knowledge.

To remediate this problem, the students may need training that emphasizes semantic knowledge along with syntactic knowledge. In particular, the students need help in building conceptual models of what goes on inside the computer when each statement is executed. Interestingly, most BASIC manuals emphasize appropriate grammar for each statement—the key word READ must be preceded

TABLE 6.9
Types of Knowledge Required for Computer Programing

Types of Knowledge	Examples from Basic
Syntactic knowledge	
Lexical units:	
line numbers	10, 20, 30, 40
key words	LET, INPUT, PRINT, IF
variable names	A, B. C
numerical values	10.2, 5, -.322
arithmetic symbols	+, -, *, /, **
logical relations	=, >, >
punctuation	(), ; : "
Combination rules:	
microrules	For every (in a statement there must be a corresponding).
macrorules	A FOR statement on one line of a program requires a NEXT statement on a subsequent line.
Semantic knowledge	
Microsemantics:	
actions	move, find, create, destroy, decide, combine, wait, allow
objects	number, program line
locations	pointer, input queue, memory space, program list, output screen, keyboard
Macrosemantics:	
do-until loop	FOR-action-NEXT module
ordering numbers	INPUT-IF-LET module
manipulating data	INPUT-LET-PRINT module

by a line number and blank space and followed by a blank space and address name or list—but barely touch on relevant conceptual models that a user might use to understand to what the statements refer.

Conceptual Model Training

Bayman (1983; Bayman & Mayer, 1988) used conceptual model training to help novice programmers understand what goes on inside the computer for each BASIC statement. She began with a standard BASIC manual that emphasized language syntax for each of 10 BASIC statements; then, she inserted information about the conceptual model underlying each statement. For example, Table 6.10 provides a section of the standard manual along with the corresponding section of a conceptual model manual. As you can see, the manuals are identical in their descriptions of language syntax for each statement, but the conceptual model includes additional information about the semantics of each statement. In particular, the manual lists the actions that are carried out on objects inside the computer for each statement.

The conceptual model training is designed to help students acquire a conceptual model of the computer as shown in Fig. 6.3. The model provides a concrete representation of several of the main functional locations in the computer includ-

TABLE 6.10
Example Sections for Concrete Model and Standard Manual

Introductory Text Common to Both Manuals for the LET Statement

In the memory of a computer there is a special area that is set aside to store values defined by the user. This area can be thought of as a group of memory spaces. Each memory space can contain only one value at a time. In most computer programing languages, the value of a variable (or a memory space) changes each time it is assigned a new value by the user. A value is assigned to a variable by using the LET statement. For practical reasons, all the variable names used throughout this minicourse will be letters of the alphabet.

Standard Manual

Now assume that you type in:

     LET A = 1   and press the RETURN key.
The value 1, will be stored in variable A.

Concrete Model Manual

Now, assume that you type in:

     LET A = 1   and press the RETURN key.
The steps the computer carries out are:

     1. *FIND* the number stored in memory space A.
     2. *ERASE* the number in memory space A.
     3. *WRITE* the number, 1, in memory space A.
     4. *WAIT* FOR the next statement to be entered from the
        keyboard.

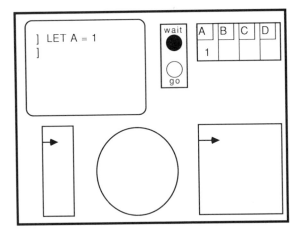

FIG. 6.3.   A conceptual model for learning BASIC computer programing.

ing an erasable memory scoreboard, a program list with pointer arrow, an output screen, an input queue with pointer arrow, a wait/run traffic light, and an erasable scratchpad for arithmetic computations. Similar models have been used in previous research (Mayer, 1981, 1989).

Like structure training for scientific problem solving and representation training for mathematical problem solving, conceptual model training is consistent with the three features of successful thinking skills programs listed in the introduction of this chapter. Conceptual model training focuses on small, component skills, that is, translating each programing statement into a concrete description of actions inside the computer. Conceptual model training emphasizes process—systematically analyzing what each statement means. Finally, conceptual model training embeds problem-solving training within the specific domain of computer programing.

Evaluation of Conceptual Model Training

To evaluate the effectiveness of conceptual model training, Bayman (1983; Bayman & Mayer, 1988) gave students a 2-hour introduction to BASIC computer programing using either a standard manual or a standard manual that was enhanced with conceptual training. After instruction, the students took retention tests, which evaluated whether they had acquired the syntactic knowledge in the standard manual and the semantic knowledge in the enhanced manual, and transfer tests to determine whether they could transfer what they learned to solve new programing problems.

To evaluate syntactic knowledge, students were given fact retention questions

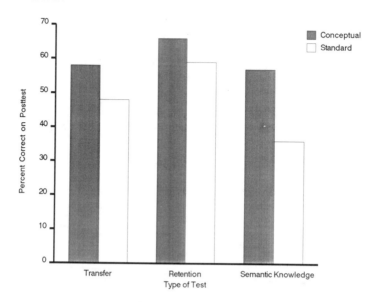

FIG. 6.4. Posttest performance of conceptual model trained and standard groups. (Note: Data based on collapsing across several versions of conceptual model training.)

such as those previously described. This can be considered a retention test because it covers material that was presented in the manual for both groups of students. To evaluate problem-solving transfer, students were asked to generate or interpret short BASIC programs such as those previously described. This can be considered a transfer test because students were not explicitly trained in how to put statements together to solve programing problems.

Does conceptual model training improve students' ability to transfer what they have learned about the statements to solving programing problems? The left portion of Fig. 6.4 summarizes the performance of the standard and conceptual model groups on retention and transfer tests. As expected, the groups did not differ on retention but the conceptual model group outperformed the standard group on problem-solving transfer. These results are consistent with the idea that conceptual model training fosters the development of meaningful learning outcomes.

Does conceptual model training improve students' semantic knowledge? To evaluate students' semantic knowledge, students were given lines of BASIC code such as "70 LET A = B + 1" and asked to list "in plain English all of the steps that the computer has to carry out in order to execute this line." An answer was scored as correct if it contained the major actions underlying the statement such as "replace the number in memory space A with the value of B + 1." As shown in the right portion of Fig. 6.4, the conceptually trained students performed much better than the standard trained students on tests of semantic knowledge. This finding helps to validate that conceptual model training was successful in improving students' semantic knowledge.

Finally, do students who possess good conceptual models of the computer transfer what they have learned better than students who possess poor models? To answer this question, Bayman compared students who scored high on the test of semantic knowledge to those who scored low. As expected, students with good conceptual models performed much better on the transfer test (75% correct) than those with poor conceptual models (42% correct). This finding helps to demonstrate a relation between acquiring underlying semantic knowledge and ability to succeed on transfer.

In summary, conceptual model training appears to be another example of teaching for thinking. Apparently, students who learned under this method developed conceptual models of the computer system that helped them to transfer what they had learned to solving of new programing problems. As in the previous exemplary training programs, the effectiveness of conceptual model training may depend on learner characteristics. In particular, conceptual model training is not effective with students who come to the classroom with strong backgrounds in mathematics and computer science. Presumably, these more able students already possess conceptual models to use in understanding new programing statements. In addition, research on expert/novice differences suggests that as students become more expert in programing, the conceptual models used for initial training may need to be replaced with more sophisticated models (Mayer, 1989).

SUMMARY

Implications for Teaching and Learning

In the introduction to this chapter, I alluded to the disappointments awaiting anyone who wants to search for teachable aspects of problem solving. In light of this context, I described three thinking-skills programs whose goals were fairly modest—to examine teaching for transfer within relatively restricted domains. Fortunately, there are several promising themes running through each of the exemplary thinking skills programs that I have described.

First, this work demonstrates that it is possible to teach in a way that fosters students' thinking. Structure training, representation training, and conceptual model training all are attempts at teaching for thinking. In each of the three programs, teaching for thinking succeeded in improving students' ability to transfer what they learned to new problem-solving situations.

Second, the common thread running through each of the programs is an emphasis on students' modeling of the comprehension process for the problem solving in specific domains. In structure training, students learned to outline scientific text based on knowledge of typical expository prose structures. Knowing the basic kinds of text structures improved students' reading comprehension processes by allowing them to focus on important information and organize the information in a way that allowed for inferences. In representation training, students learned how to translate mathematical word problems by using concrete diagrams. Knowing how to phrase the sentences in a word problem allowed students to focus on important information in the problem and to organize the information in a useful way. In conceptual model training, students learned to translate programming statements into descriptions of what goes on inside the computer. Knowing how to use a conceptual model helped students to understand the relationships among statements so they could generate and comprehend programs.

Third, although each training program emphasized comprehension processes, the traditional training for each subject matter area does not. Typically, students are not taught how to organize scientific text, how to translate word problems into diagrams, or how to build conceptual models for computer programing. Similarly, each of the training programs was intended to improve problem-solving transfer whereas the traditional emphasis in many subject matter areas is on retention of the presented information. Thus had we evaluated the effectiveness of our programs based solely on retention, we would not have found strong positive evidence. In short, the payoff for helping students to become better comprehenders of problems lies in transfer rather than retention.

We are left with some tantalizing implications for anyone interested in research or practice in the teaching of thinking. Traditionally, educational programs have emphasized producing correct answers, whereas our research suggests that improvements in thinking are achieved through an emphasis on the processes by which answers are produced. Traditionally, improvements in intellectual performance have been attributed to strengthening of some sort of monolithic ability, whereas, our research suggests that improvements in thinking come about through instruction in small, component intellectual skills such as comprehension processes. Finally, teaching of thinking has sometimes been taught as a separate subject matter area—isolated from other subject matter—whereas, research on transfer suggests that we should integrate teaching for thinking within specific subject domains such as mathematics, science, or computer programing (Cormier & Hagman, 1987; Mayer, 1987b).

Suggestions for Future Research

Research on teaching of thinking skills in the sciences and mathematics requires a fruitful interaction between those interested in developing psychological theories of human cognition and those interested in developing school curricula that serve the needs of students. Two important criteria for future research are: (a) that studies test basic theories of human learning and cognition, and (b) that studies take place within the context of real students learning science and mathematics within real educational settings. Instead of theory-based research within contrived or aritificial settings or classroom research that lacks theoretical focus, future research on the teaching of thinking should be both theoretical and practical.

An excellent example of theory-based research within a real educational setting comes from a recent study by Elawar (in press). On a theoretical side, Elawar based her instruction on Mayer's (1987a) componential theory of mathematical problem solving; on the practical side, she taught predominantly Hispanic sixth-grade students how to solve arithmetic word problems within the context of their regular classroom over the course of 30 class sessions. Her results show that students in the experimental classrooms achieve a much greater pretest-to-posttest gain in mathematical problem-solving performance and in positive attitudes toward mathematical problem solving than students in the control classrooms. Although research by Lewis (1989a, 1989b)—as described in this chapter—demonstrated that mathematical problem solving could be improved via representation training in a highly controlled and short-term situation, Elawar's research has extended the research arena for teaching of thinking skills into a real functioning mathematical classroom over the long-term.

In summary, questions about the teachability of thinking skills challenge researchers to develop a more complete understanding of the conditions for transfer of problem-solving skills and challenge educators to develop a curriculum that has a place for thinking. In answering questions about the teachability of thinking skills, we can advance both our psychological theories of human problem solving and the educational practices of our schools. It is important that answers to these questions be based on solid research evidence and well-documented psychological theories rather than on educational fads.

ACKNOWLEDGMENTS

An earlier version of this chapter was presented as a G. Stanley Hall Lecture at the 96th Annual Meeting of the American Psychological Association, Atlanta, Georgia, August 12–16, 1988 and was published in *The Stanley Hall Lecture Series, Volume 9*. Copyright © 1989 by the American Psychological Association. Adapted by permission.

The research description of structure training in science is based on a doctoral dissertation by Cook (1982) titled, "Instructional Effects of Text-Structure Based Reading Strategies on the Comprehension of Scientific Prose." The research description on representational training in mathematics is based on a doctoral dissertation by Lewis (1989a), titled "Effects of Representation Training on Students' Comprehension of Relational Statements in Arithmetic Word Problems." The research description of concrete model training in computer programing is based on a doctoral dissertation by Bayman (1983), titled "Effects of Instructional Procedures on Learning a First Programming Language."

7

Cognitive Research on Thinking in Academic Science and Mathematics: Implications for Practice and Policy

Audrey B. Champagne
University at Albany, State University of New York

Contributors to this volume, cognitive scientists and educational researchers in the cognitive tradition, join the already substantial public and professional chorus critical of the quality of school science and mathematics. Government officials and business and industrial leaders cite the inadequacies of public education, in particular, the poor quality of science and mathematics education. The inferior performance of American youth on national and international tests of scientific and mathematical literacy has serious implications for the future of our democratic form of government and for the United States' competitiveness in the world market. Dispersed throughout the many recommendations to strengthen public education are references to the potential of cognitive science to enhance the quality of school science and mathematics.

THE COGNITIVE CONCEPTUALIZATION OF SCIENTIFIC AND MATHEMATICAL THINKING

Cognitive research on scientific and mathematical thinking has two broad objectives: to describe the cognitive attributes of skilled performance and to discover the mechanisms of their development. The work of Glaser (chap. 4) and Greeno (chap. 3) that is reported in this volume follows in the scientific tradition of the naturalists, their goal to describe cognitive capabilities of various populations. Glaser collects experts from endeavors as diverse as chess and radiology to describe how the organization of their knowledge and processing strategies differ from those of novices, while Greeno collects instances of implicit understanding of scientific and mathematical concepts and principles in young people and in individuals without formal education in science or mathematics. Mayer is the theorist, his goal to investigate how the development of thinking can be enhanced via formal instruction. Halpern, Van Haneghan, and Mestre are the engineers, drawing on the theories and empirical work of the scientists to develop strategies to enhance desirable intellectual performance.

These researchers criticize the conventional approach to teaching science and mathematics, which emphasizes the transmission of factual information and rote procedures applied to inappropriate problems, allows little opportunity for students to engage in scientific or mathematical thinking, and produces inert knowledge and thinking skills limited to a narrow range of academic problems. Based on their research, they recommend:

1. Educational practice based on theoretical models of knowledge structures and processing strategies that students are expected to develop;
2. Teachers use tasks more like those that students encounter in daily life to teach and assess science and mathematics achievement; and
3. Educators design formal educational settings that encourage active intellectual engagement in scientific and mathematical thinking.

These recommendations will become part of educational practice only after incorporation into national and state policy and translation into curriculum materials and pedagogical strategies.

EDUCATIONAL POLICY FORMULATION

Educational policy is formulated at the national, state, and local levels. National policy makers' assessment of the potential of cognitive research to raise achievement scores in science and mathematics will determine the place of cognitive science in the nation's educational research and development agenda. Based on their assessment, policy makers set the level of support for: (a) basic (theory-driven) cognitive research; (b) curriculum and assessment development that applies cognitive theory; and (c) educational research (practice-driven) conceptualized in the cognitive perspective.

Policy makers determine level of resource allocation on the basis of conclusions drawn from the analysis of propositions of the following type:

1. Poor science and mathematics achievement is not due to lack of knowledge of how to teach, but rather to contextual factors such as:
   (a) declining resources available for education because of a weak economy;
   (b) a culture that does not value academic excellence;

(c) poorly motivated students;

(d) assessment instruments that emphasize information recall;

(e) an overladed curriculum; and

(f) poorly prepared and overworked teachers.

2. Poor science and mathematics achievement is not due to inadequate theory, but rather the failure to translate the theory into practice.

3. The potential of cognitive research to improve science and mathematics achievement is greater than the potential of research in other fields of psychology, the social sciences, or education.

These propositions are typical of those examined by policy makers at the state level who decide the role of cognitive theory, if any, in the education of science and mathematics teachers and in mandated curricula and assessment instruments.

Policy alternatives consistent with Proposition 1 include: (a) redistributing tax dollars from less critical areas to education; (b) allocating funds to address and redress social ills; (c) allocating funds to strengthen assessment; (d) allocating funds to reduce the content of the school curriculum; or (e) allocating funds to underwrite teacher education.

Assigning priorities to contextual variables is one complexity of educational policy formulation. Should limited federal resources be allocated to on-the-job training or to public education? Should resources be allocated to community efforts to change the attitudes of the nation's youth toward drugs and the value of formal education? Is federal money better spent on basic research or on providing incentives to encourage the most able college graduates to teach? Basic research is only one of a multitude of social, political, and economic forces that factor into educational policy and as such must compete with them for scarce resources.

Policy makers who concur with Proposition 2 will allocate more resources to educational development than to basic research in behavioral or social science but must decide whether the resources should go directly to schools or to developers at universities and free-standing educational research and development (R&D) organizations. Providing resources for materials development directly to schools has certain advantages. Teachers have ownership of material they develop themselves so the problems and expense of implementation of externally developed materials are avoided. The disadvantage is that teachers are not well informed about behavioral and social theory or skillful in its application. A large portion of the nation's science and mathematics teachers have been in the classroom for as many as 30 years (Darling-Hammond, 1984) and have had little opportunity to become informed about recent developments in the social and behavioral sciences theory or to practice its application to pedagogy. Even teachers who have been exposed to these ideas have had little opportunity to develop design skills, nor is there any time in the hectic school day to devote to designing teaching materials. If teachers are expected to apply theory to practice, they need to be knowledgeable about educationally relevant theory, skillful in its application, and have time to devote to design.

The alternative to materials design at the school level is educational materials development at institutions of higher education and educational R&D organizations. This alternative is not without its weaknesses. Past experience has demonstrated that materials designed outside the school setting without the participation of experienced teachers reflect neither classroom constraints, nor the concerns of teachers. Science and mathematics materials designed during the educational crisis of the 1960s were not widely implemented nor distributed by mainstream educational publishing houses. This experience has influenced the development policies of the federal government (Shamos, 1989). The National Science Foundation's new wave of science materials development required partnerships of schools, developers, and publishers. Shifting the responsibility of development closer to the schools and consequently away from the research community reduces the likelihood of the application of theory in the design process.

Policy makers who concur with Proposition 3, will favor allocation of more resources to basic R&D in the cognitive framework. A policy to support one branch of research in preference to others requires careful consideration. For both intellectual and practical reasons, a balance of research support across the behavioral and social sciences makes good sense. The stance of the scientific community on this matter is that resources for research should be distributed across disciplines based on the scientific quality of the research and its potential to contribute to theory. The research's potential to contribute to practice should not be a funding factor. Even so, in policy formulation, practical matters and politics influence allocations for basic research.

Even from a practical perspective, a balanced research portfolio is reasonable. There is no evidence that any one field of social or behavioral research has had more influence on educational practice than any other. Developmental, cognitive, and behavioral psychology as well as sociology and anthropology have contributed to educational practice. The incorporation of theory into curriculum materials should be encouraged. Materials that incorporate theory possess greater intellectual integrity than those based on conventional wisdom and unexamined experience. The use of theory in the design of educational materials encourages reexamination of conventional practice. However, policy makers are well advised to be cautious about limiting resources to developers based on the application of a certain theory. These recommendations and cautions are equally applicable at the state level.

In addition to the allocation of resources, policy makers also influence the quality of science and mathematics education via national and state assessments and state curriculum frameworks. If, indeed, scientific and mathematical thinking are valued outcomes of science and mathematics education, then policy makers need to send clear signals of these priorities in the content of curriculum frameworks and assessment instruments. The emphasis on thinking in curriculum frameworks and on assessment instruments must be commensurate with the value placed on thinking as an outcome of science and mathematics education. Furthermore, the contents of frameworks and assessments must be consistent not only with good science and mathematics but also with practices consistent with behavioral and social theory.

COGNITIVE THEORY

Responsible policy formulation requires assessment of the potential contributions of basic research to educational practice. A thorough assessment includes a review of the empirical basis of the theory, the validity of the underlying assumptions, and the theory's applicability to the practice of school science and mathematics.

The Empirical Basis

The recommendations for classroom practice proposed in this volume are based on research using a diverse collection of intellectual tasks performed by individuals of widely varying ages, experience, and formal education (see Table 7.1). Inferences about contents of mind—declarative knowledge structures and information processing capabilities—are based on observations of performance. Some studies are descriptive, others contrast performance of (a) representatives drawn from different populations or (b) subjects who have been exposed to experimental treatments.

Intellectual Tasks.   The tasks are drawn from three domains—academe, the world outside of school, and research. Academic tasks are those that educators use to teach and to test. Examples include performing laboratory exercises, reading text, and solving end-of-chapter exercises. Real-world tasks are those that are encountered in personal, civic, or professional life—making change at the grocery store, interpreting blue prints, or reading x-rays. Experimental research tasks are those contrived by social and behavioral scientists to tap some aspect of human thinking. Piagetian tasks and the interpretation of the operation of the function machine reported by Greeno are examples of experimental tasks. The performance of academic tasks calls upon a variety of skills and academic disciplines including reading, writing, computation, observation, and inferring in mathematics and the natural sciences—biology, chemistry, and physics.

A category of task, not a part of the empirical base discussed in this volume are those intellectually challenging tasks typical of those engaged in by scientists and mathematicians pushing back the frontiers of knowledge—a category of tasks called *inquiry* in the literature of science and mathematics. Glaser calls these tasks problems of discovery or ill-structured problems.

TABLE 7.1
Populations and Intellectual Tasks

Populations	Intellectual Task
GLASER	
Chess masters	Recall the configuration of a chess board
Electronic technicians	Recall circuit diagrams
Radiologists	Recognize abnormalities on x-rays
Physicists	Sort academic physics problems
Physicists	Retrieve related equations
Physicists	Preliminary analysis of textbook physics problems
Algebra students	Detect physically impossible situations in word problems
GREENO	
Seventh graders	Analysis of mechanical function machine
Untutored workers (youngsters and adults)	Perform work-related tasks—Carrying out street sales transactions, filling dairy orders, interpreting a blue print
MAYER	
Junior college students	Distinguish science text structure
College students	Solving abgebra word problems
Novices	Program in BASIC
MESTRE	
College students (who have completed classical mechanics)	Solve academic physics problems (from Resnick and Halliday)
VAN HANEGHEN	
Fourth, fifth, and 6th grade students	Solve proportional reasoning and rate problems embedded in adventure stories
HALPERN	
College students	Solve algebraic rate problems
13-year-olds	Interpret the results of a word problem requiring division
College students	Piagetian tasks

Experimental Populations. The studies reported in this volume were conducted with subjects of widely varying ages and educational experience. Ages of subjects range from elementary school children to middle-aged physicists and chess masters. Educational experiences of the subjects range from no formal education to graduate studies in the natural sciences.

The Theory

The theory derived from these empirical studies has both descriptive and causal elements. The descriptive elements consist of models of the contents of mind—

the declarative and procedural knowledge that underlie the performance of intellectual tasks. The causal elements include propositions that relate the quality of performance to the nature of the performers' declarative and procedural knowledge and proposes hypotheses about the conditions under which the knowledge structures and mental processes develop.

Models. The models that comprise the descriptive elements of cognitive theory are based on the performance of experts in the academic disciplines, professions, and games (chess). Although the tasks on which the models are developed are called problems in the research reports, in most cases the tasks are routine; that is, the experts are either performing a task they have performed previously or a task that taps some component part of a well-practiced task. The tasks on which the models are based are not the kind that experts engage in the most demanding aspects of their professional lives.[1] For instance, for the PhD physicist, sorting end-of-chapter problems from a college physics textbook is a task of quite a different level of challenge from the task of analyzing a laser-produced spectra to infer the fine structure of a complex organic molecule. The sorting task may not be familiar—the physicist has not engaged in it previously—but neither is it challenging. That is, it requires only the application of a component process—problem representation—of the usual procedure for solving end-of-chapter problems followed by sorting the problems according to similarity of representation.[2] In contrast, the spectra analysis task is one that challenges the physicist's intellectual powers. The structure of the molecule under investigation is unknown and the theoretical relationship of the peaks and valleys of the spectra with the energetics of electronic transformations in the molecule are complex. Matching features of the spectra with the many possible transformations is a multifactor task making this research task a true problem for the researcher in the conventional meaning of the word.

This distinction is critical to cognitive theory. Inferences about the contents of mind based on observations of performance must be tempered by the difficulty of the task for the performer as well as the performer's familiarity with the task. When the task is unfamiliar, observations provide insights into a different type of mental processes than do observations of the performance of a familiar or unchallenging task. These mental processes are those, as Glaser describes, that characterize the mental processes of experts engaging in ill-structured problems.

In those instances where the task is neither familiar nor challenging familiar, engagement is little more than an automatic response, which calls upon well-practiced low-level mental processes. Engaging a task of this sort in all likelihood has little effect on the content or structure of declarative knowledge. However, when engagement in a task calls for restructuring mental processes or

---

[1]The exception reported in this volume is physicians reading x-rays.

[2]This assumes that the physicists in the study are engaged both in teaching and research as a frequently engaged in the solution of end-of-chapter problems.

requires relating information not previously associated in that particular way, engaging in the task produces learning—that is, new processing strategies and knowledge structures develop. The development of new mental strategies, honing existing processes, adding new information to existing knowledge structures, or rearrangement of existing structures are instances of learning. When the task is repeated, practice may either serve to maintain a certain performance level, without changing mental processes or knowledge structures, or practice may hone mental skills and result in the reorganization knowledge structures to produce learning.

Because engagement in a challenging task can produce learning, the distinction blurs between task performance that serves as a window into the existing state of mind and task performance that produces changes in the mind state. This, in turn, blurs the scientific distinction among the terms thinking, problem solving, and learning, which are used to characterize the tasks as well as the mental processes used to develop the theoretical models.

Domain Knowledge and Mental Processes.   A consistent theme throughout the chapters in this volume is the interaction of information and mental processes during the performance of intellectual tasks. The research reported in this volume as well as other work by cognitive researchers underscores the idea that both are essential. Glaser describes the contributions of domain knowledge to component skills of experts, namely pattern perception, problem representation, and qualitative reasoning. Mayer acknowledges the contribution of domain knowledge to academic thinking skills. The common feature of the strategies Mayer reports for training academic thinking skills is to build a knowledge structure on which mental processes operate. In the case of teaching junior college students to outline scientific text, they were first taught expository prose structure. The ability to interpret and write computer programs in BASIC were developed by first teaching students the structure and function of computers on which the program operates.

The Nature of the Knowledge Base.   Cognitive theory proposes that successful task performance requires a rich hierarchically structured knowledge base, but does not address how the knowledge base develops. Mayer and Mestre apply very different strategies. Mayer's strategy is to build the knowledge base by feeding information into the system. In contrast, Mestre seeks to structure the knowledge base by engaging the students in problem-solving activities.

Inert Knowledge.   Greeno's paper draws attention to another facet of the relationship between thinking and knowledge. Greeno discusses, in a cognitive theoretical framework, an idea about the nature of knowledge that is closely related to Whitehead's philosophical construct, inert knowledge. Inert knowledge cannot be applied in contexts other than the formal context in which it was learned. Greeno discusses research demonstrating that the context in which knowledge develops influences the extent to which the knowledge can be applied in other contexts. Greeno describes instances of thinking by individuals not formally trained in mathematics that shares features of formal mathematical reasoning. This reasoning is exhibited in situations that are both familiar and essential to the individual's economic well-being. Other research studies demonstrate the inability of individuals to apply their knowledge of mathematical principles learned under formal conditions in real-world contexts—that is, outside the classroom. This suggests that when learning occurs in rich contexts the knowledge base contains information that facilitates application of the knowledge.

THEORY INTO PRACTICE

The congruence of cognitive theory with the features of educational practice determines in large measure the degree to which theory becomes translated into practice. Cognitive theory addresses limited aspects of the practice of science and mathematics education and, even in its range of applicability, certain ambiguities and apparent contradictions in the theory make its translation problematic.

Categories of Thinking

One particularly problematic feature is the poor definition of the territory of thinking. This ambiguity is not limited to cognitive theory; in fact, it is a characteristic that psychology shares with education. The professional literature of psychology and education, even the chapters in this volume, contain a bewildering array of terms for thinking skills associated with science and mathematics. Except in reports of empirical studies, the terms are not defined operationally, that is, by describing the process for measuring them. Neither is there any system for categorizing the terms or specifying the relationships among them.

One dimension of the nature of thinking is complexity. The operative term that appears frequently in the literature is *order*. Some thinking skills are higher order, some are lower order. However, the characteristics that distinguish these two types of thinking remains elusive. Is the distinction a matter of qualitative and quantitative differences? Are higher order skills concatenations of lower order skills or are they qualitatively different (as in concrete operational and formal operational thinking)? Or is the distinction:

- a matter of age—is children's reasoning lower order because it is less abstract and concatenations composed of fewer component skills than the thinking of adults?

- a matter of experience and formal education—is the auto mechanic's thinking lower order because it is less abstract than the engineer's, even though both are composed concatenations of equally large numbers of component skills?

- a matter of difficulty in teaching or learning—is lower order thinking easily taught to all, whereas higher order thinking is learned only by a small portion of the population?

- a matter of the frequency of occurrence in the general population—is thinking higher order because only a small portion of the population exhibits it?

- a matter of performance facility—is thinking lower order if it can be performed quickly and unconsciously?

Thinking is also implicitly categorized according to the breadth of its applicability, that is, whether it is generic, task specific, or discipline specific. Thus, problem solving may be a generic skill, specific to a kind of task—problems, for instance—or specific to a discipline—such as science or mathematics.

Perhaps the most perplexing feature of the cognitive perspective is the blurring of the distinction between thinking, a mental process, and tasks that are used to engender or to test those processes. For example, the phrase, problem solving, refers both to a kind of task and the mental processes used to complete the task.

The complexity of the relationships among different aspects of thinking is evident in the three taxonomies—A, B, and C—that represent different relationships among the many terms used for thinking (see Fig. 7.1). Taxonomy A is a categorization based on order, Taxonomy B is a categorization based on thinking processes, and Taxonomy C is a categorization of academic and assessment exercises used to teach and test thinking. Although these taxonomies are incomplete, they organize the various terms used for thinking in a way that illuminates its many attributes, which are not well incorporated in contemporary cognitive theory. Until these attributes of different forms of thinking are better defined, their relationships to each other better understood, and the mechanisms of their development incorporated into performance and learning theory, the application of theory to practice will be hindered.

Authentic Tasks

A feature of cognitive theory that recently has received considerable attention is the relationships of the nature of intellectual tasks and the thinking skills that engagement in them produces. The work of Van Haneghan is based on the principle that active engagement by the learner in authentic or real-world tasks facilitates the development of thinking skills. Various features of authentic tasks and the relationship of these features to the skills they develop are proposed by the authors in this volume. Halpern postulates that an essential feature of real-world tasks is that often they are worked on by groups of people. She conjectures that working in groups increases time on task, referring to a study by Treisman (1985), where students working in groups spent more time on tasks and learned more, to support her position. Also, she proposes that the group setting broadens the knowledge and experience that can be brought to bear on the task, which should facilitate successful engagement.

Van Haneghan proposes that the nature of the task environment is an essential feature. His theory is that a rich environment—even if it is fictional—provides clues that facilitate the solution of problems. This conclusion is supported by a study of weight watchers conducted by Lave (1988). She reported observing a weight watcher use objects in his environment to measure a portion of cottage cheese that was three-quarters of two-thirds of a cup. Even though he had studied calculus, the man did not apply the school-learned algorithm for taking a fractional part of a fraction to solve the problem; rather he used objects in the environment.

Greeno suggests two other features of authentic tasks that facilitate learning—one is the representation of mathematical and scientific relationships in physical objects; the other is the relevance of the task to the performer. The observation that construction workers are more skilled in applying proportional reasoning in the interpretation of blueprints than students who learned the principles in formal mathematics, for instance, can be explained by the presence of physical objects in the builders environment that serve as physical representations of the symbols in the blueprint (Carraher, 1986).

Tasks are more relevant to students when they involve physical objects or relate to something students already know. Mayer applied this principle when he taught the function of the computer to facilitate programing skill development. The use of analogy and metaphor are ways in which to relate new ideas to existing knowledge structure. Tasks also gain relevance when successful performance contributes to personal survival or well-being. This aspect of relevance is illustrated in the study reported by Carraher, Carraher, and Schliemann (1985). For the Brazilian street vendor, the successful performance of making change is motivated by the need for economic survival.

The notion of authentic or real-world tasks has considerable appeal, as evidenced by its prevalence in the contemporary rhetoric of assessment. If the construct (authenticity) is to effect deep change in educational practice—either teaching or testing—much better understanding of the causal mechanisms that produce learning needs to be established. Is simply putting kids in groups enough? Are physical objects the critical element? Or is it simply a matter of selecting the right rewards? A coherent theory at a sufficient level of detail will facilitate the translation of this interesting construct of cognitive theory into practice.

Taxonomy A

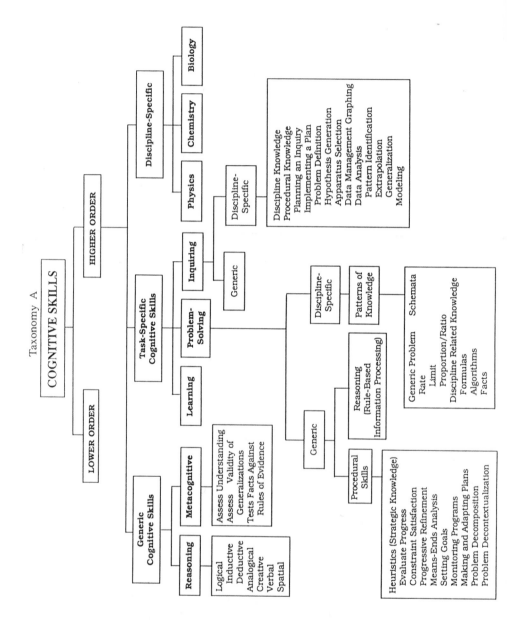

Taxonomy B

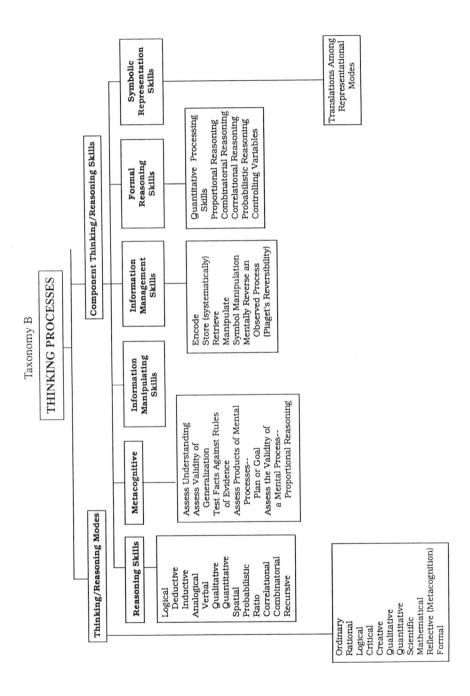

Taxonomy C

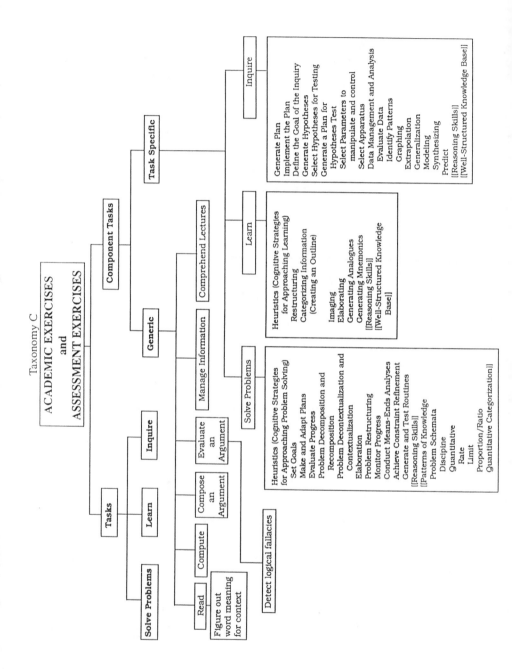

Training or Construction

The chapters in this volume pose an interesting contradiction regarding instructional approaches to the development of scientific and mathematical thinking. Although the authors criticize the procedural approaches to teaching mathematics and science typical of conventional school practice, the strategies they propose to train thinking skills are procedural. Halpern, for instance, presents a problem-solving framework adapting problem-solving *procedures* proposed by Polya. She also concludes from a report on a study by Schoenfeld (1985) that "After only five *training* sessions practicing these strategies, the students who received this training were performing significantly better than a comparable control group who did not receive *training* with these general problem-solving skills" [emphasis added](Halpern, chap. 2 in this volume). Similarly, Mayer " . . . opts for . . . helping students to model the *process* by which an expert thinks about solving scientific, mathematical, or programing problems" [emphasis added] (Mayer, chap. 6 in this volume). Mestre's chapter reports on an approach to teaching problem solving "in which novices practiced performing problem analyses similar to those performed by experts" (Mestre et al., chap. 5 in this volume).

This approach to thinking, which is both procedural and has the goal of training procedures, stands in stark contrast to the approach proposed by Greeno (chap. 3 in this volume):

> The findings that I have sketched here . . . suggests an approach to mathematics learning that would turn the usual curriculum on its head. It would involve constructing situations that support mathematical thinking by students, in groups and as individuals, and would provide them [the opportunity] to construct mathematical ideas meaningfully as part of their mathematical thinking.

According to Greeno's view, the teachers' responsibility is to create an environment in which the students can engage in interesting intellectual tasks. The student constructs thinking strategies for successful completion of the tasks as the result of engagement. In contrast, the procedures training approach is consistent with the view that the teachers' or the computers' responsibility is to transmit the procedures to students.

The theoretical rationale underlying studies of procedures training to enhance thinking is based on work reported by Glaser, who concludes: "Experts knowledge is highly *procedural* and goal-oriented." The theoretical justification of procedural training studies is not a cognitive theory of learning but rather a cognitive theory of performance. There is a serious mismatch between the nature of the tasks on which the performance theory is based and the tasks that science and mathematics educators expect students to engage successfully. Although the theory derives from expert's performance on tasks that are routine for the expert, the educational objective is to produce thinking skills that enable students to engage successfully in tasks that are nonroutine for the students. The practical consequence is procedural training of procedures that neglects precisely those thinking processes required for engagement in nonroutine problems. If instructional strategies are to be based on performance theory, the performance theory should be derived from studies using the tasks and populations for whom the teaching strategies are intended. The existing cognitive theory of performance needs to be enriched by studies of successful and unsuccessful students, contrasting the knowledge and mental processes that distinguish successful *learning* performance.

The foregoing assumes that models describing state of cognition are an appropriate theoretical basis for the design of instruction. This assumption bears critical examination. Logically, a theory of learning—of the mechanisms that produce changes in cognitive states—is more appropriate.

In the absence of a cognitive theory of learning, the practitioner must resolve the contradiction. Should practitioners continue providing didactic instruction in procedures, albeit more sophisticated procedures, or engage small groups of students in authentic tasks? Should practitioners assume that thinking skills can be trained or that students engaged in authentic tasks will construct effective approaches for themselves?

Even though extant performance theory is somewhat limited in its applicability to the design of instruction, it is nonetheless useful in the definition of instructional goals and in the diagnosis of flawed performance. The skilled practitioner with appropriate caution can use descriptive models of expert performance to define cognitive outcomes for science and mathematics education. Furthermore, the skilled practitioner can match a student's performance against the theoretical model as a means of generating plausible hypotheses about missing knowledge or process skills that plausibly account for flawed performance (Burton & Brown, 1978).

CONCLUSIONS

For cognitive theory in particular and social/behavioral theory in general to realize its promise, researchers need to take more responsibility for helping policy makers and practitioners understand better the strengths as well as the limitations of the theory. Also, researchers must exercise restraint in making recommendations and claims. Recommendations should be congruent with the theory and claims tempered by the complexity of the variables that contribute to the development of thinking.

Policy makers and practitioners alike bear responsibility for being informed about relevant social and behavioral theory and for engaging in critical analysis of the researcher's recommendations and claims. Practitioners also have the responsibility for providing feedback to researchers informed by the experience of applying the theory to the design of instructional materials and strategies and to classroom practice. Policy makers should carefully consider Mayer's (chap. 6 in this volume) observation that Research on teaching of thinking skills in the sciences and mathematics . . . "requires a fruitful interaction between those interested in developing psychological theories of human cognition and those interested in developing school curricula that serve the needs of students" and incorporate opportunities for this kind of interaction in educational policy initiatives.

References

Anderson, J. R., Boyle, C. F., & Yost, G. (1985). The geometry tutor. *Proceeding of the International Joint Conference in Artificial Intelligence* (pp. 1–7). Los Angeles.

Anderson, J. R., Farrell, R., & Sauers, R. (1984). Learning to program in LISP. *Cognitive Science, 8*, 87–129.

Asimov, I. (1989, March 31). Combatting U. S. scientific illiteracy. *Los Angeles Times, Part V*, 8.

Bank Street College of Education. (1985). *Voyage of the Mimi.* Pleasantville, NY: Sunburst Communications.

Bartholomae, D. (1985). Inventing the university. In M. Rose (Ed.), *When a writer can't write: Studies in writer's block and other composing-process problems* (pp. 134–165). New York: Guilford Press.

Bayman, P. (1983). *Effects of instructional procedures on learning a first programming language.* Unpublished doctoral dissertation, University of California, Santa Barbara.

Bayman, P., & Mayer, R. E. (1988). Using conceptual models to teach BASIC computer programming. *Journal of Educational Psychology, 80*, 291–298.

Bayman, P., & Mayer, R. E. (1983). Diagnosis of beginning programmers' misconceptions of BASIC programming statements. *Communications of the ACM, 26*, 519–521.

Bransford, J. D., Franks, J. J., Vye, N. J. & Sherwood, R. D. (1989). New approaches to instruction: Because wisdom can't be told. In S. Vosniadou & A. Ortony (Eds.), *Similarity and analogical reasoning* (pp. 470–497). New York: Cambridge University Press.

Bransford, J. D., Goin, L. I., Hasselbring, T. S., Kinzer, C. K., Sherwood, R. D., & Williams, S. M. (1988). Learning with technology: Theoretical and empirical perspectives. *Peabody Journal of Education, 64*, 5–26.

Bransford, J., Hasselbring, T., Barron, B., Kulewicz, S., Littlefield, J., & Goin, L. (1988). Uses of macro-contexts to facilitate mathematical thinking. In R. Charles & E. A. Silver (Eds.), *The teaching and assessing of mathematical problem solving* (pp. 125–147). Hillsdale, NJ: Lawrence Erlbaum Associates.

Bransford, J., Kinzer C., Risko, V., Rowe, D., & Vye, N. (1989). Designing invitations to thinking: Some initial thoughts. In S. McCormick & J. Zutell (Eds.), *Cognitive and social perspectives for literacy research and instruction* (pp. 35–54). Chicago, IL: The National Reading Conference.

Bransford, J., Sherwood, R., & Hasselbring, T. (1988). The video revolution and its effects development: Some initial thoughts. In G. Foreman & P. Pufall (Eds.), *Constructivism in the computer age* (pp. 173–201). Hillsdale, NJ: Lawrence Erlbaum Associates.

Bransford, J., Sherwood, R., Kinzer, C., & Hasselbring, T. (1985). *Havens for learning: Toward a framework for developing effective uses of technology* (Technical Report No. 85.1.1). Nashville, TN: Vanderbilt University.

Bransford, J. D., Sherwood, R. S., Hasselbring, T. S., Kinzer, C. K., & Williams, S. M. (1990). Anchored Instruction: Why we need it and how technology can help. In D. Nix & R. Spiro (Eds.), *Cognition, education, and multimedia: Exploring ideas in high technology* (pp. 115–141). Hillsdale, NJ: Lawrence Erlbaum Associates.

Bransford, J. D., & Stein, B. S. (1984). *The ideal problem solver: A guide for improving thinking, learning, and creativity.* New York: Freeman.

Bransford, J. D., Vye, N., Kinzer, C., & Risko, V. (1990). Teaching thinking and content knowledge: Toward an integrated approach. In B. F. Jones & L. Idol (Eds.), *Dimensions of thinking and cognitive instruction* (pp. 381–413). Hillsdale, NJ: Lawrence Erlbaum Associates.

Bridwell, L. S. (1980). Revising strategies in twelfth grade students' transactional writing. *Research in the Teaching of English, 14,* 197–222.

Brophy, J., & Goode, T. (1986). Teacher behavior and student achievement. In M. C. Wittrock (Ed.), *Handbook of research on teaching* (pp. 328–375). New York: Macmillan.

Brown, A., & Campione, J. (in press). Communities of learning and thinking, or a context by any other name. *Human Development.*

Brown, A. L. & Palincsar, A. (1989). Guided, cooperative learning and individual knowledge acquisition. In L. B. Resnick (Ed.), *Knowing and learning: Essays in honor of Robert Glaser* (pp. 393–451). Hillsdale, NJ: Lawrence Erlbaum Associates.

Brown, J. S., & Burton, R. R. (1978). Diagnostic models for procedural bugs in basic mathematical skills. *Cognitive Science, 12,* 155–192.

Brown, J. S., Collins, A., & Duguid, P. (1989). Situated cognition and the culture of learning. *Educational Researcher, 17,* 32–41.

Bullock, M., Gelman, R., & Baillergeon, R. (1982). The development of causal reasoning. In W. J. Friedman (Ed.), *The developmental psychology of time* (pp. 209–254). New York: Academic Press.

Carey, S. (1985). *Conceptual change in childhood.* Cambridge, MA: MIT Press/Bradford Books.

Carpenter, T. P., & Moser, J. M. (1982). The development of addition and subtraction problem-solving skills. In T. P. Carpenter, J. M. Moser, & T. A. Romberg (Eds.), *Addition and subtraction: A cognitive perspective* (pp. 9–24). Hillsdale, NJ: Lawrence Erlbaum Associates.

Carpenter, T. P., & Moser, J. M. (1983). The acquisition of addition and subtraction concepts. In R. Lesh & M. Landau (Eds.), *Acquisition of mathematics concepts and processes* (pp. 7–44). New York: Academic Press.

Carraher, T. N. (1986). From drawings to buildings: Working with mathematical scales. *International Journal of Behavioral Development, 9,* 527–544.

Carraher, T. N., Carraher, D. W., & Schliemann, A. D. (1985). Mathematics in the streets and the schools. *British Journal of Developmental Psychology, 3,* 21–29.

Catrambone, R., & Holyoak, K. J. (1987, November). *Procedural variability and transfer in problem solving.* Paper presented at the 28th annual meeting of the Psychonomic Society, Seattle, WA.

Champagne, A. B., & Klopfer, L. E. (1981). Problem solving as outcome and method in science teaching: Insights from 60 years of experience. *School Science and Mathematics, 81,* 3–8.

Chance, P. (1986). *Thinking in the classroom: A survey of programs.* New York: Columbia University Teacher's College Press.

Chase, W. G., & Simon, H. A. (1973). Perception in chess. *Cognitive Psychology, 4,* 55–81.

Chi, M. T. H., Bassok, M., Lewis, M. W., Reimann, P., & Glaser, R. (1989). Self-explanations: How students study and use examples in learning to solve problems. *Cognitive Science, 13,* 145–182.

Chi, M. T. H., Feltovich, P. J., & Glaser, R. (1981). Categorization and representation of physics problems by experts and novices. *Cognitive Science*, *5*, 121–152.

Chi, M. T. H., Glaser, R., & Rees, E. (1982). Expertise in problem solving. In R. J. Sternberg (Ed.), *Advances in the psychology of human intelligence* (pp. 7–70). Hillsdale, NJ: Lawrence Erlbaum Associates.

Clancey, W. J. (1986). From Guidon to Neomycin and Hercules in twenty short lessons: ONR final report 1979–1985. *AI Magazine*, *7*, 40–60.

Clark, M. J., & Halpern, D. F. (1990). *The million dollar question: Can an intensive learning experience improve success for lowest quartile students?* Manuscript submitted.

Cognition and Technology Group at Vanderbilt. (1990). Anchored instruction and its relationship to situated cognition. *Educational Researcher*, *19*(6), 2–10.

Collea, F. P., & Nummedal, S. (1980). *Development of reasoning in science (DORIS): A course in abstract thinking* (Tech. Rep.). Fullerton, CA: School of Mathematics, Science, and Engineering.

Collins, A., Brown, J. S., & Newman, S. E. (1989). Cognitive apprenticeship: Teaching the crafts of reading, writing, and mathematics. In L. B. Resnick (Ed.), *Knowing, learning, and instruction: Essays in honor of Robert Glaser* (pp. 453–494). Hillsdale, NJ: Lawrence Erlbaum Associates.

Cook, L. K. (1982). *Instructional effects of text structure-based reading strategies on the comprehension of scientific prose.* Unpublished doctoral dissertation, University of California, Santa Barbara.

Cook, L. K., & Mayer, R. E. (1988). Teaching readers about the structure of scientific text. *Journal of Educational Psychology*, *80*, 448–456.

Cormier, S. M., & Hagman, J. D. (Eds.) (1987). *Transfer of learning: Contemporary research and applications.* San Diego: Academic Press.

Dansereau, D. F., Collins, K. W., McDonald, B. A., Holley, C. D., Garland, J., Diekoff, G., & Evans, S. H. (1979). Development and evaluation of a learning strategy training program. *Journal of Educational Psychology*, *71*, 64–73.

Darling-Hammond, L. (1984). *Beyond the commission reports: The coming crisis in teaching.* Santa Monica, CA: Rand Corporation.

DeCorte, E., & Verschaffel, L. (1985). Beginning first graders' initial representation of arithmetic word problems. *Journal of Mathematical Behavior*, *4*, 3–21.

de Groot, A. (1965). *Thought and choice in chess.* The Hague: Mouton.

de Groot, A. (1966). Perception and memory versus thought: Some old ideas and recent findings. In B. Kleinmuntz (Ed.), *Problem solving* (pp. 19–50). New York: Wiley.

De Loughry, T. J. (1989, February 22). Reports hits U.S. students' inability to grasp complex tasks. *The Chronicle of Higher Education*, *35*, A2.

Detterman, D. K., & Sternberg, R. J. (Eds.). (1982). *How and how much can intelligence be increased.* Norwood, NJ: Ablex.

diSessa, A. A. (1983). Phenomenology and the evolution of intuition. In D. Gentner & A. Stevens (Eds.), *Mental models* (pp. 15–33). Hillsdale, NJ: Lawrence Erlbaum Associates.

Dreyfus, T. (1983). The function concept in college students: Linearity, smoothness and periodicity. *Focus on Learning Problems in Mathematics*, *5*, 119–132.

Egan, D., & Schwartz, B. (1979). Chunking in recall of symbolic drawings. *Memory and Cognition*, *7*, 149–158.

Elawar, M. (in press). Effects of teaching metacognitive skills to students with low mathematical ability. *Contemporary Educational Psychology*.

Eylon, B. S., & Reif, F. (1984). Effects of knowledge organization on task performance. *Cognition and Instruction*, *1*, 5–44.

Fawcett, H. P. (1938). *The nature of proof, the thirteenth yearbook of the National Council of Teachers of Mathematics.* New York: Teachers College, Columbia University.

Flower, L., Hayes, J. R., Carey, L., Schriver, K., & Stratman, J. (1986). Detection, diagnosis, and the strategies of revision. *College Composition and Communications*, *37*, 16–55.

Fox, L. S., Marsh, G., & Crandall, J. C., Jr. (1983, April). *The effect of classroom experiences on formal operational thinking.* Paper presented at the annual meeting of the Western Psychological Association, San Francisco, CA.

Frederiksen, J. R., & Collins, A. (1989). A systems approach to educational testing. *Educational Researcher 18,* 27–32.

Furman, L., Montavon, E., Barron, B., Vye, N., Bransford, J., Hasselbring, T., & Shah, P. (1989, April). *The effects of problem formulation training and type of feedback on math handicapped students' problem solving abilities.* Paper presented at the meeting of the American Educational Association, San Francisco.

Gardner, M., Greeno, J. G., Reif, F., Schoenfeld, A. H., diSessa, A. A., & Stage, E. (Eds.) (1990). *Toward a scientific practice of science education.* Hillsdale, NJ: Lawrence Erlbaum Associates.

Gelman, R., & Gallistel, C. R. (1978). *The child's understanding of number.* Cambridge, MA: Harvard University Press.

Gelman, R., & Greeno, J. G. (1989). On the nature of competence: Principles for understanding in domains. In L. B. Resnick (Ed.), *Knowing, learning, and instruction: Essays in honor of Robert Glaser.* Hillsdale, NJ: Lawrence Erlbaum Associates.

Gelman, R., & Meck, E. (1986). The notion of principle: The case of counting. In J. Hiebert (Ed.), *Conceptual and procedural knowledge: The case of mathematics.* Hillsdale, NJ: Lawrence Erlbaum Associates.

Glaser, R. (1981). The future of testing: A research agenda for cognitive psychology and psychometrics. *American Psychologist, 36,* 923–936.

Glaser, R., & Bassok, M. (1989). Learning theory and the study of instruction. *Annual Review of Psychology, 40,* 631–666.

Greeno, J. G. (1988). The situated activities of learning and knowing mathematics. *Proceedings of the tenth annual meeting of the North American Chapter of the International Group for the Psychology of Mathematics Education.* DeKalb, IL: Northern Illinois University.

Greeno, J. G. (1991). A view of mathematical problem solving in school. In M. U. Smith (Ed.), *Toward a unified view of problem solving: Values from the content domains* (pp. 69–88). Hillsdale, NJ: Lawrence Erlbaum Associates.

Greeno, J. G., Magone, M. E., Rabinowitz, M., Ranney, M., Strauch, C., & Vitolo, T. M. (1985). *Investigations of a cognitive skill* (Rep. No. 1985/27). Learning Research and Development Center, University of Pittsburgh.

Greeno, J. G., & Moore, J. L. (1990). *Implicit understanding of quantitative functions in physical systems.* Center for Research in Education, Stanford University.

Greeno, J. G., & Simon, H. A. (1988). Problem solving and reasoning. In R. C. Atkinson, R. Herrnstein, G. Lindzey, & R. D. Luce (Eds.), *Stevens' handbook of experimental psychology* (pp. 589–672). New York: Wiley.

Griffiths, D. H. (1976). Physics teaching: Does it hinder intellectual development? *American Journal of Physics, 44,* 81–85.

Halpern, D. F. (1986a). *Sex differences in cognitive abilities.* Hillsdale, NJ: Lawrence Erlbaum Associates.

Halpern, D. F. (1986b) A different answer to the question, "Do sex differences in spatial abilities exist?" *American Psychologist, 41,* 1014–1015.

Halpern, D. F. (1987a). Analogies as a critical thinking skill. In D. Berger, K. Pezdek, & W. Banks (Eds.), *Applications of cognitive psychology: Computing and education* (pp. 75–86). Hillsdale, NJ: Lawrence Erlbaum Associates.

Halpern, D. F. (1987b). Critical thinking across the curriculum: Methods and strategies to promote critical thinking in every classroom. In M. Heiman & J. Slomianko (Eds.), *Thinking skills: Concepts and techniques.* (pp. 69–76). Washington, D.C.: National Education Association.

Halpern, D. F. (1989a). The disappearance of cognitive gender differences: What you see depends on where you look. *American Psychologist, 44,* 1156–1158.

Halpern, D. F. (1989b). *Thought and knowledge: An introduction to critical thinking* (2nd ed.). Hillsdale, NJ: Lawrence Erlbaum Associates.

Halpern, D. F. (in press). *Sex differences in cognitive abilities* (2nd ed.). Hillsdale, NJ: Lawrence Erlbaum Associates.

Hardiman, P. T., Dufresne, R. & Mestre, J. (1989). The relationship between problem categorization and problem solving among experts and novices. *Memory and Cognition, 17,* 627–638.

Hatano, G., & Inagaki, K. (1986). Two courses of expertise. In H. Stevenson, H. Azuma, & K. Hakuta (Eds.), *Child development and education in Japan* (pp. 262–272). New York: W. H. Freeman.

Hatano, G., & Inagaki, K. (in press). Sharing cognition through collective comprehension activity. In L. B. Resnick (Ed.), *Socially shared cognition.* New York: W. H. Freeman.

Hayes, J. R., & Simon, H. A. (1976). The understanding process: Problem isomorphs. *Cognitive Psychology, 8,* 165–190.

Heller, J. I., & Reif, F. (1984). Prescribing effective human problem solving processes: Problem description in physics. *Cognition and Instruction, 1,* 177–216.

Herrnstein, R. J., Nickerson, R. S., de Sanchez, M., & Swets, J. A. (1986). Teaching thinking skills. *American Psychologist, 41,* 1279–1289.

Hiebert, J., & LeFevre, P. (1986). Conceptual and procedural knowledge in mathematics: An introductory analysis. In J. Hiebert (Ed.), *Conceptual and procedural knowledge: The case of mathematics* (pp. 1–27). Hillsdale, NJ: Lawrence Erlbaum Associates.

Hinsley, D. A., Hayes, J. R., & Simon, H. A. (1977). From words to equations: Meaning and representation in algebra word problems. In M. A. Just & P. A. Carpenter (Eds.), *Cognitive processes in comprehension* (pp. 89–106). Hillsdale, NJ: Lawrence Erlbaum Associates.

Inhelder, B., & Piaget, J. (1958). *The growth of logical thinking from childhood to adolescence.* New York: Basic Books.

Janvier, C. (1978). *The interpretation of complex Cartesian graphs representing situations: Studies and teaching experiments.* Unpublished doctoral dissertation, University of Nottingham.

Johnson, R. T. J. (1987). *The ability to retell a story: Effects of adult mediation context on children's story recall and comprehension.* Thesis, Vanderbilt University, Nashville, TN.

Johnson-Laird, P. N., (1983). *Mental models.* Cambridge, MA: Harvard University Press.

Kouba, V. L., Brown, C. A., Carpenter, T. P., Lindquist, M. M., Silver, E. A., & Swafford, J. O. (1988). Results of the fourth NAEP assessment of mathematics: Number, operations, and word problems. *Arithmetic Teacher, 35,* 14–19.

Kuhn, S. E. (1989, Spring). How business helps schools, *Fortune,* pp. 91–106.

Lampert, M. (1986). Knowing, doing, and teaching multiplication. *Cognition and Instruction, 3,* 305–343.

Lampert, M. (1990). When the problem is not the question and the solution is not the answer: Mathematical knowing and teaching. *American Educational Research Journal, 27,* 29–64.

Larkin, J. H. (1979). Processing information for effective problem solving. *Engineering Education, 70,* 285–288.

Larkin, J. H. (1981). Enriching formal knowledge: A model for learning to solve problems in physics. In J. R. Anderson (Ed.), *Cognitive skills and their acquisition* (pp. 311–334). Hillsdale, NJ: Lawrence Erlbaum Associates.

Larkin, J. H. (1983). The role of problem representation in physics. In D. Gentner & A. L. Stevens (Eds.), *Mental models.* Hillsdale, NJ: Lawrence Erlbaum Associates.

Larkin, J. H., McDermott, J., Simon, D. P., & Simon, H. A. (1980a). Expert and novice performance in solving physics problems. *Science, 208,* 1335–1342.

Larkin, J., McDermott, J., Simon, D. P. & Simon, H. A. (1980b). Models of competence in solving physics problems. *Cognitive Science, 4,* 317–345.

Lave, J. (1988). *Cognition in practice.* Cambridge: Cambridge University Press.

Lave, J., Murtaugh, M., & de la Rocha, O. (1984). The dialectic of arithmetic in grocery shopping.

In B. Rogoff & J. Lave (Eds.), *Everyday cognition: Its development in social context* (pp. 67–94). Cambridge, MA: Harvard University Press.

Lesgold, A., Rubinson, H., Feltovich, P., Glaser, R., Klopfer, D., & Wang, Y. (1988). Expertise in a complex skill: Diagnosing x-ray pictures. In M. T. H. Chi, R. Glaser, & M. Farr(Eds.), *The nature of expertise* (pp. 311–432). Hillsdale, NJ: Lawrence Erlbaum Associates.

Lesh, R. (1981). Applied mathematical problem solving. *Educational Studies in Mathematics, 12,* 235–264.

Lester, F. J., & Garofalo, J. (1982, April). *Metacognitive aspects of elementary school student's performance on arithmetic tasks.* Paper presented at the annual meeting of the American Educational Research Association, New York.

Lewis, A. B. (1989a). *Effects of representation training on students' comprehension of relational statements in arithmetic word problems.* Unpublished doctoral dissertation, University of California, Santa Barbara.

Lewis, A. B. (1989b). Effects of training on students' representation of compare arithmetic word problems. *Journal of Educational Psychology, 81,* 521–531.

Lewis, A. B. & Mayer, R. E. (1987). Students' misconception of relational statements in arithmetic word problems. *Journal of Educational Psychology, 79,* 363–371.

Lewis, M. W., Milson, R., & Anderson, J. R. (1988). Designing an intelligent authoring system for high school mathematics ICAI: The teacher apprentice project. In G. Kearsley (Ed.), *Artificial intelligence and instruction: Applications and methods.* New York: Addison-Wesley.

Lipman, M. (1985). Thinking skills fostered by philosophy for children. In J. Segal, S. Chipman, & R. Glaser (Eds.), *Thinking and learning skills: Relating instruction to basic research* (Vol. 1, pp. 83–108). Hillsdale, NJ: Lawrence Erlbaum Associates.

Lochhead, J. (1983). The mathematical needs of students in the physical sciences. In A. Ralston & G. S. Young (Eds.), *The future of college mathematics* (pp. 55–70). New York: Springer-Verlag.

Mayer, R. E. (1981). The psychology of how novices learn computer programming. *Computing Surveys, 13,* 121–141.

Mayer, R. E. (1982). Memory for algebra story problems. *Journal of Educational Psychology, 74,* 199–216.

Mayer, R. E. (1983). *Thinking, problem solving, cognition.* New York: Freeman.

Mayer, R. E. (1985a). Mathematical ability. In R. J. Sternberg (Ed.), *Human abilities: An information processing approach* (pp. 127–150). New York: Freeman.

Mayer, R. E. (1985b). Learning in complex domains: A cognitive analysis of computer programming. In G. Bower (Ed.), *Psychology of learning and motivation* (Vol. 19, pp. 89–130). New York: Academic Press.

Mayer, R. E. (1986). Mathematics. In R. F. Dillon & R. J. Sternberg (Eds.), *Cognition and instruction* (pp. 127–154). New York: Academic Press.

Mayer, R. E. (1987a). *Educational psychology: A cognitive approach.* Boston: Little, Brown.

Mayer, R. E. (1987b). The elusive search for teachable aspects of problem solving. In J. A. Glover & R. R. Ronning (Eds.), *Historical foundations of educational psychology* (pp. 327–348). New York: Plenum Press.

Mayer, R. E. (1987c). Instructional variables that influence cognitive processing during reading. In B. K. Britton & S. Glynn (Eds.), *Executive control processes in reading* (pp. 127–216). Hillsdale, NJ: Lawrence Erlbaum Associates.

Mayer, R. E. (1988, August). *Teaching for thinking: Research on the teachability of thinking skills.* G. Stanley Hall Lecture presented at the annual meeting of the American Psychological Association, Atlanta, GA.

Mayer, R. E. (1988). From novice to expert. In M. Halendar (Ed.), *Handbook of human computer interaction* (Vol. 6, pp. 569–580). Amsterdam: Elseiver Scientific.

Mayer, R. E. (1989). Models for understanding. *Review of Educational Research, 59,* 43–64.

Mayer, R. E., Larkin, J. H., & Kahane, J. B. (1984). A cognitive analysis of mathematical problem solving ability. In R. J. Sternberg (Ed.), *Advances in the psychology of human intelligence* Vol. 2, pp. 321–373). Hillsdale, NJ: Lawrence Erlbaum Associates.

McCloskey, M. (1983). Naive physical theories. In D. Gentner & A. Stevens (Eds.), *Mental models* (pp. 299–324). Hillsdale, NJ: Lawrence Erlbaum Associates.

McDermott, J., & Larkin, J. H. (1978). Re-representing textbook physics problems. In *Proceedings of the 2nd National Conference of the Canadian Society for Computational Studies of Intelligence* (pp. 156–164). Toronto: University of Toronto Press.

McKinnon, J. W. (1976). The college student and formal operations. In J. W. Renner, G. D. Stafford, A. E. Lawson, J. W. McKinnon, F. E. Friot, & D. H. Kellogg (Eds.), *Research, training and learning with the Piaget model* (pp. 110–129). Norman: University of Oklahoma Press.

McMillen, L. (1989, July 5). Clare Luce Booth Fund to spend $3.5-million a year to encourage women to study and teach science. *The Chronicle of Higher Education, 35,* A23.

McNamara, T. P., Miller, D. L., & Bransford, J. D. (1991). Mental models and reading comprehension. In T. D. Pearson, R. Barr, M. Kamil & P. Mosenthal (Eds.), *Handbook of reading research.* (Vol. 2, pp. 490–511). New York: Longman.

Mestre, J., Dufresne, R., Gerace, W., & Hardiman, P. (1988). Hierarchical problem solving as a means of promoting expertise. In *Proceedings of the Tenth Annual Conference of the Cognitive Science Society* (pp. 312–318). Hillsdale, NJ: Lawrence Erlbaum Associates.

National Council of Teachers of Mathematics (1989). *Curriculum and evaluation standards for school mathematics.* Reston, VA: Author.

National Research Council (1989). *Everybody counts: A report to the nation on the future of mathematics education.* Washington, DC: National Academy Press.

National Science Foundation (1989). *Report on the National Science Foundation disciplinary workshops on undergraduate education.* Washington, DC: Author.

Newell, A., & Simon, H. A. (1972). *Human problem solving.* Englewood Cliffs, NJ: Prentice-Hall.

Nickerson, R. S., Perkins, S. N., & Smith, E. E. (Eds.) (1985). *The teaching of thinking.* Hillsdale, NJ: Lawrence Erlbaum Associates.

Paige, J. M., & Simon, H. A. (1966). Cognitive processes in solving algebra word problems. In B. Kleinmuntz (Ed.), *Problem solving* (pp. 51–118). New York: Wiley.

Pea, R. D. (1988). *Distributed intelligence in learning and reasoning processes.* Paper presented at the meeting of the Cognitive Science Society, Montreal.

Pea, R., & Greeno, J. G. (1990). *Reflections on directions of reform in mathematics education.* Presented at the meeting of the American Educational Research Association. Boston.

Piaget, J., Grize, J., Szeminska, A., & Bang, V. (1977). *The psychology and epistemology of functions.* (Original work published in 1968.)

Polya, G. (1945). *How to solve it: A new aspect of mathematical method.* New York: Doubleday.

Polya, G. (1957). *How to solve it.* Princeton, NJ: Princeton University Press.

Porter, A. (1989). A curriculum out of balance: The case of elementary school mathematics. *Educational Researcher, 18,* 9–15.

Renner, J. S. (1976). What this research says to schools. In J. W. Renner, G. D. Stafford, A. E. Lawson, J. W. McKinnon, F. E. Friot, & D. H. Kellogg (Eds.), *Research, training and learning with the Piaget model* (pp. 174–191). Norman: University of Oklahoma Press.

Resnick, R., & Halliday, D. (1977). *Physics.* New York: Wiley.

Saxe, G. B. (1988). Candy selling and math learning. *Educational Researcher, 17,* 14–21.

Saxe, G. B. (1990). The interplay between children's learning in school and out-of-school contexts. In M. Gardner, J. G. Greeno, F. Reif, A. H. Schoenfeld, A. A. diSessa, & E. Stage (Eds.), *Toward a scientific practice of science education* (pp. 219–234). Hillsdale, NJ: Lawrence Erlbaum Associates.

Schneider, W. (1985). Training high performance skills: Fallacies and guidelines. *Human Factors, 27,* 285–300.

Schoenfeld, A. H. (1985). *Mathematical problem solving.* New York: Academic Press.

Schoenfeld, A. H. (1987). What's all the fuss about metacognition? In A. H. Schoenfeld (Ed.), *Cognitive science and mathematics education.* Hillsdale, NJ: Lawrence Erlbaum Associates.

Schoenfield, A. H. (1987). (Ed.). *Cognitive science and mathematics education.* Hillsdale, NJ: Lawrence Erlbaum Associates.

Schoenfeld, A. H., Arcavi, A., & Smith, J. (in press). Learning: The microgenetic analysis of one student's understanding of a complex subject matter domain. In R. Glaser (Ed.), *Advances in instructional psychology* (Vol. 4). Hillsdale, NJ: Lawrence Erlbaum Associates.

Schoenfeld, A., & Herrmann, D. J. (1982). Problem perception and knowledge structure in expert and novice mathematical problem solvers. *Journal of Experimental Psychology: Learning, Memory and Cognition, 8,* 484–494.

Scribner, S. (1984). Studying working intelligence. In B. Rogoff & J. Lave (Eds.), *Everyday cognition: Its development in social context.* Cambridge, MA: Harvard University Press.

Segal, J. W., Chipman, S. F., & Glaser, R. (Eds.) (1985). *Thinking and learning skills: Vol. 1, Relating instruction to research.* Hillsdale, NJ: Lawrence Erlbaum Associates.

Shamos, M. H. (1989). Views of scientific literacy in elementary school science programs: Past, present, and future. In A. B. Champagne, B. E. Lovitts, & B. J. Calinger (Eds.), *This year in school science 1989: Scientific literary* (pp. 109–127). Washington, D.C.: American Association for the Advancement of Science.

Sherwood, R., Kinzer, C., Hasselbring, T., & Bransford, J. (1987). Macro-contexts for learning: Initial findings and issues. *Journal of Applied Cognition, 1,* 93–108.

Silver, E. A. (Ed.) (1985). *Teaching and learning mathematical problem solving.* Hillsdale, NJ: Lawrence Erlbaum Associates.

Silver, E. A. (1986). Using conceptual and procedural knowledge: A focus on relationships. In J. Hiebert (Ed.), *Conceptual and procedural knowledge: The case of mathematics* (pp. 181–198). Hillsdale, NJ: Lawrence Erlbaum Associates.

Sime, M. (1973). *A child's eye view: Piaget for young parents and teachers.* New York: Harper & Row.

Simon, D. P., & Simon, H. A. (1978). Individual differences in solving physics problems. In R. Siegler (Ed.), *Children's thinking: What develops?* (pp. 325–348). Hillsdale, NJ: Lawrence Erlbaum Associates.

Simon, H. A. (1973). The structure of ill-structured problems. *Artificial Intelligence, 4,* 181–201.

Smith, M. U. (Ed.) (1991). *Toward a unified theory of problem solving: Views from the content domains.* Hillsdale, NJ: Lawrence Erlbaum Associates.

Smith, W. S., Frazier, N. I., Ward, S., & Webb, F. (1983). Early adolescent girls and boys learning of a spatial-visual skill—replications. *Journal of Education, 67,* 239–243.

Sprafkin, C., Serbin, L. A., Denier, C., & Connor, J. M. (1983). Cognitive consequences and early interventions. In M. Liss (Ed.), *Social and cognitive skills* (pp. 167–192). New York: Academic Press.

Steen, L. A. (1987). Mathematics education: A predictor of scientific competitiveness. *Science, 237,* 251–252.

Stein, N. L., & Glenn, C. G. (1979). An analysis of story comprehension in elementary school children. In R. Freedle (Ed.), *Advances in discourse processes* (Vol. 2). Hillsdale, NJ: Lawrence Erlbaum Associates.

Sweller, J. (1988). Cognitive load during problem solving: Effects on learning. *Cognitive Science, 12,* 257–285.

Touger, J., Dufresne, R., Gerace, W., & Mestre, J. (1987). Hierarchical organization of knowledge and coherent explanation in the domain of elementary mechanics. In J. Novak (Ed.), *Proceedings of the second International Seminar on Misconceptions and Educational Strategies in Science and mathematics.* Ithaca, NY: Cornell University, Department of Education.

Treisman, P. U. (1985). *A study of mathematics performance of black students at the University of California, Berkeley.* Unpublished doctoral dissertation.

Van Haneghan, J. P., & Baker, L. (1989). Cognitive monitoring in mathematics. In C. B. McCormick, G. Miller, & M. Pressley (Eds.), *Cognitive strategy research: From basic research to educational applications* (pp. 215–238). New York: Springer–Verlag.

Voss, J. F., & Post, T. A. (1988). On the solving of ill-structured problems. In M. T. H. Chi, R. Glaser, & M. Farr (Eds.), *The nature of expertise* (pp. 261–286). Hillsdale, NJ: Lawrence Erlbaum Associates.

Vye, N., Bransford, J., Furman, L., Barron, B., Montavon, E., Young, M., Van Haneghan, J., & Barron, L. (1989, April). *An analysis of students' mathematical problem solving in real world settings.* Paper presented at the meeting of the American Educational Research Association, San Francisco.

Vygotsky, L. S. (1978). *Mind in society: The development of higher psychological processes.* Cambridge, MA: Harvard University Press.

Wagner, S., & Kieran, C. (Eds.) (1989). *Research issues in the learning and teaching of algebra.* Hillsdale, NJ: Lawrence Erlbaum Associates.

Wellman, H. M., & Estes, D. (1986). Early understanding of mental entities: A reexamination of childhood realism. *Child Development, 57,* 910–923.

Wheeler, D. D., & Dember, W. N. (Eds.) (1979). *A practicum in thinking.* Cincinnati, OH: University of Cincinnati.

White, B. Y., & Frederiksen, J. R. (1986). *Progressions of quantitative models as a foundation for intelligent learning environments* (Tech. Rep. No. 6277). Cambridge, MA: Bolt, Beranek & Newman.

Whitehead, A. N. (1929). *The aims of education.* New York: Macmillan.

Author Index

Subject Index

A

Abstract representation, in problem solving, 4, 5
Abstract thinking skills
  development of, 9, 10
  educational programs to develop, 10, 11
Achievement, mathematical, 1, 15
Algebra, word problems in, 66
Anchored instruction, 17, 18
Apprenticeship learning, 18
Arithmetic
  problem solving in, 16, 17
  see also Mathematics; Word problems in mathematics
Asian-American students, 3

B

Bank Street College of Education, 23
BASIC, *see* Computer programming

C

Categorization of problems, 82-88
  deep structure used for, 82-84
  principles used for, 84-87
Cognitive map, 4, 5
Cognitive psychology and research, 117-133
  categories of thinking and, 125, 126
  educational policy formulation and, 118-121

  empirical basis for theory in, 121, 122
  experimental populations used in, 122
  inert knowledge and, 124, 125
  instructional strategies in physics and, 77, 93, 94
  intellectual tasks used in, 121, 122
  models used in, 123, 124
  objectives of, 117
  recommendations based on, 118, 131, 132
  teaching thinking skills and, 1, 2, 13, 14, 98
  theories on acquiring and using information and, 5
Collaboration, *see* Group approach
College
  Collaborative mathematical thinking in, 57
  Piaget's theories incorporated into curriculum of, 10, 11
  thinking skills and enrollment in, 1
  videodiscs for instruction in, 19, 20
Competence, and practice, 72
Computer-based educational programs, 11
  Equation Sorting Tool (EST), 78, 81, 82, 88-90
  Hierarchical Analysis Tool (HAT), 78-81, 88-93
Computer programming
  conceptual model training for, 110-113